Alex CRAWFORD & Phil H. LISTEMANN

Colour artwork: Malcolm Laird

Layout & project design: Phil Listemann

Copyright © Phil Listemann 2008
Revised edition 2012

ISBN 978-29526381-8-0

Printed in France

ACKNOWLEDGEMENTS

Tom Eeles, Chris Goss, Jim Grant (Text Consultant), Hugh Halliday, Phil Jarrett, Paul Sortehaug, Ray Sturtivant, Andrew Thomas, Chris Thomas.

Edited and printed by Phil H. Listemann

philedition@wanadoo.fr

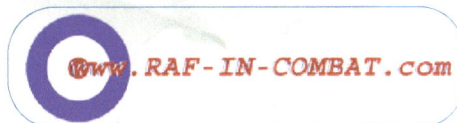

GLOSSARY OF TERMS

DFC : Distinguished Flying Cross	RCAF : Royal Canadian Air Force
DSO : Distinguished Service Order	RH : Rhodesian
Eva : Evaded	RNZAF : Royal New Zealand Air Force
F/L : Flight Lieutenant	SA : South African
F/O : Flying Officer	SAAF : South African Air Force
F/Sgt : Flight Sergeant	Sgt : Sergeant
(IRE)/RAF : Irish (from Eire) serving in the RAF	S/L : Squadron Leader
ORB : Operations Record Book	Sqn : Squadron
OTU : Operational Training Unit	W/C : Wing Commander
P/O : Pilot Officer	W/O : Warrant Officer
PoW : Prisoner of War	
RAAF : Royal Australian Air Force	
RAF : Royal Air Force	

INTRODUCTION

A photograph of the first prototype, L6844, taken shortly before its first flight in October 1938. *(Phil Jarrett)*

The Westland Whirlwind belongs to that category of aircraft which entered production but failed to live up to their designers' expectations. Its unreliable engines can be seen as a major reason for this but it only serves to hide other serious problems. Indeed, even with better engines the results would probably have been the same, as the concept of a twin-engined fighter aircraft capable of meeting single-engined fighters escorting bombers formations on an equal footing was fallacious, as combat in WW2 was soon to prove. Its American counterpart, the Lockheed P-38 Lightning, a far more powerful and superior fighter, was unable to contend with single-engined enemy fighters and after heavy losses had to relinquish this role to the P-47 and P-51. The P-38 was transferred to the role of fighter-bomber where it found a new lease of life.

The Whirlwind was produced only in very small numbers but it too was soon withdrawn from pure interception duties.

A NEW FIGHTER FOR THE FIGHTER COMMAND
In 1934 the Air Ministry launched a series of specifications aimed at providing a new monoplane fighter to replace the ageing biplanes then in RAF service. Indeed the expansion of the RAF, which had begun in 1935, was not simply concerned with increasing the numbers of aircraft in service but producing a number of new types of aircraft to equip the large number of newly formed squadrons and re-equip the ones already in service with RAF Fighter Command. Among the new specifications was the F.37/35 which called for a single-seat day and night fighter armed with cannons with a speed,

A very nice photograph of the first prototype showing its pure aerodynamic contours. The cockpit, with its all-round view, was one of the best features of the Whirlwind. *(Phil Jarrett)*

rate of climb and ceiling well in excess of contemporary, and future bomber performances. Boulton Paul, Bristol, Hawker, Supermarine and Westland produced proposals to meet F.37/35 and eventually Westland won the competition with its P.9. Two prototypes, L6844 and L6845, were ordered on 11 February 1937 against contract No.556965/36 and the type was soon named "Whirlwind". The first prototype was completed in late September 1938 and was an elegant twin-engined aircraft which looked more like a racer than a warplane. The Whirlwind introduced some advanced features, such as Fowler flaps, a new method using electron castings and magnesium alloy skinning. Initial ground handling and taxi trials began on 4 October 1938, and the first flight was made a few days later on the 11th, and fight testing began immediately.

From the beginning the Whirlwind was designed to be armed with four 20 mm cannons, a very powerful armament at that time. As a twin-engined fighter the armament could be concentrated in the nose of the aircraft giving an impressive concentration of fire power on targets, which were expected to be bombers, coming from the Continent.

However problems arose with the engines, Rolls-Royce Peregrines, which were experiencing recurrent overheating troubles. Also, with the new engineering and design concepts suffering from problems the Whirlwind's development programme began to experience delays. More problematical were its handling characteristics, including the lack of directional control, tail buffeting at the stall, and the ailerons which were considered to be too heavy. Meanwhile the RAE test programme continued but at a very slow level with only 25 hours of flying having been completed by April 1939. Worse was to follow as the number of modifications needed

rose to 250! By that time the second prototype had made its first flight, on 29 March 1939, and joined the test programme. Nevertheless a confirmed order (contract No.980384/39) for 200 Whirlwind Mk.Is was placed and these received the serial numbers P6966-P7015 (50), P7035-P7064 (30), P7089-P7128 (40), P7158-P7177 (20), P7192-P7221 (30) and P7240-P7269 (30). A second contract (No.20186/39) for another 200 aircraft followed later in the year and these received serial numbers R4243-R4283 (41), R4296-R4325 (30), R4345-R4384 (40), R4400-R4445 (46), R4460-R4479 (20), R4499-R4521 (23).

Development testing continued during the summer of 1939 while the construction of the first production aircraft began, however the engines continued to be troublesome and eventually Royce-Rolls announced, in August 1939, the termination of the Peregrine and Vulture engine programmes to focus on the development of the Merlin which was showing great promise. Consequently the Air Ministry cancelled the second batch of Whirlwinds and reduced the first order to just 114 aircraft. A total of 116 Whirlwinds were built and the last was taken on charge in January 1942.

INSTRUCTIONAL OR MAINTENANCE AIRFRAME

3063M : L6844 - April 1942
3497M : P6967 - April 1943

A view of the starboard side of L6845, the second prototype. In this photograph the relatively large engine nacelles are clearly shown. While under construction L6845 incorporated some improvements and further modifications resulting from the testing of L6844. *(Phil Jarrett)*

Whirlwind P7048 taken during a flight test. The cannons are still to be installed. *(Phil Jarrett)*

TECHNICAL DATA
WHIRLWIND MK.I (FIGHTER)

Manufacturer and production:
116 by Westland

Type:
Single-seater fighter/fighter-bomber.

Accomodation:
One pilot

Power plant:
Two Rolls-Royce liquid-cooled twelve-cylinder 885 hp
Peregrine I.

Fuel & Oil
Fuel (Imp Gal):
134 [612,5 l]
(one 24 and one 43 Gal tanks in each wing)

Oil (Imp Gal) per engine:
Standard : 5 [23 l]

Dimensions:
Span : 32 ft 3-in [9,83 m]
Length : 45 ft 0-in [13,72 m]
Height : 16 ft 3-in [4,95 m]
Wing area : 250 Sq ft [23,23 m²]

Weights:
Empty : 8,310 lb [3 370 kg]
MTOW : 10,379 lb [4 710 kg],
& 11,411 lb [5 180 kg]
as fighter bomber

Performance:
Max speed:
360 mph at 15,000 ft
[580 km/h at 4 570 m]

Cruising speed: 210 mph [340 km/h]
Rate of climb: 1,550 ft/min [474 m/min]
Service ceiling: 30,300 ft [9 250 m]
Range: 630 miles [1 000 km]
Endurance at cruising speed: 1h30

Armament:
4 x 20mm Hispano cannon with 60rpg

provision for
2 x 500 lb [227 kg] bombs under the wings

DELIVERIES AND STRENGHT

Month (at last day)	Delivered	Total delivered	Op. Losses	Accident [1]	SOC	Available
by March 1939	2	2	-	-	-	2
May 40	1	3	-	-	-	3
June 40	1	4	-	-	-	4
July 40	3	7	-	-	-	7
August 40	1	8	-	1	-	7
September 40	3	11	-	-	-	10
October 40	2	13	-	-	-	12
November 40	6	19	-	-	-	18
December 40	2	21	2	1	-	17
January 41	6	27	-	1	-	22
February 41	9	36	1	-	-	30
March 41	4	40	2	-	-	32
April 41	18	58	1	2	-	47
May 41	11	69	-	1	-	57
June 41	12	81	-	2	-	67
July 41	12	93	-	1	-	78
August 41	8	101	-	-	-	86
September 41	6	107	3	1	-	88
October 41	3	110	2	3	-	86
November 41	2	112	2	-	-	86
December 41	3	115	-	1	-	88
January 42	1	116	-	1	-	88
February 42	-	116	4	-	-	84
March 42	-	116	-	3	-	81
April 42	-	116	-	2	1	78
May 42	-	116	2	1	-	75
June 42	-	116	1	1	1	72
July 42	-	116	2	-	-	70
August 42	-	116	-	-	-	70
September 42	-	116	-	1	-	69
October 42	-	116	4	1	-	64
November 42	-	116	1	-	-	63
December 42	-	116	3	-	-	60
January 43	-	116	3	1	-	56
February 43	-	116	3	2	-	51
March 43	-	116	1	1	-	49
April 43	-	116	7	1	1	40
May 43	-	116	4	2	1	33
June 43	-	116	2	-	-	31
July 43	-	116	-	1	-	30
August 43	-	116	-	2	-	28
September 43	-	116	1	1	-	26
October 43	-	116	3	-	2	21
November 43	-	116	-	-	1	20
December 43	-	116	-	-	1	19
January 44	-	116	-	1	3	15
.../...						
July 44	-	116	-	-	3	12
../..						
September 44	-	116	-	-	12	-

[1] In case of accident, the month of the accident was selected above the struck of charge date (SOC).

THE UNITS

Three Whirlwinds, HE-V/P6969, HE-J/P6985, and HE-L /P6987, flying in formation at the beginning of 1941. These were the first production aircraft to reach No.263 Squadron. (*IWM CH.5000*)

No.263 Squadron
code : HE
July 1940 - December 1943

The first unit selected to operate the Whirlwind was No.25 Squadron, a night fighter unit, so far equiped with Blenheim Mk.Is. In May, the Squadron received two Whirlwinds for evaluation as night fighters, but the experiment was shortlive and the Squadron was converted to Beaufighter instead.

FIRST WHIRLWIND SQUADRON

On 10 June 1940, two days after the loss of HMS *Glorious* No.263 Squadron was reformed at Drem, Scotland. They were the first squadron to receive the RAF's latest fighter the twin engine Westland Whirlwind. Production problems with the Peregrine engines led to a delay so a number of Hurricanes were issued to the squadron as a stop gap measure.

The first Whirlwind, P6966, reached the squadron on 6 July 1940. This aircraft was flown in by the Squadron's new commander, Squadron Eeles. A week later another two arrived but the very next day one of them was damaged in a forced landing. As expected with new aircraft there were a number of problems with the engines and the airframe. In addition the four 20mm cannon were prone to jamming.

The Whirlwinds were formed into C Flight under the command of Flight Lieutenant Smith, the other flights flying Hurricanes. This flight was to develop the Whirlwind and iron out any of its bugs. As with the previous month training continued with most days seeing aircraft in the air. Pilots were still familiarising themselves on the Whirlwind, although C Flight still remained non-operational. Training continued to be the norm for most days. The Whirlwind flight was eventually disbanded and the

Squadron reverted back to the normal two flights. A Flight became the developing flight with the Whirlwinds, B flight keeping its Hurricanes. On 7 August 1940 the first Whirlwind P6966 was lost. During take off Pilot Officer McDermot suffered a burst tyre. Informed that the undercarriage had suffered damage he baled out near Stirling.

Squadron Leader H.Eeeles became the first Commanding Officer of a Whirlwind unit. His task was to bring the squadron up to operational status and he left the unit after successfully completing this. (*Tom Eeles*)

Work up and Operations

The Squadron moved to Drem on the South side of the Firth of Forth on 2 September 1940. Here they were in an ideal position to defend the naval base at Rosyth. While day and night patrols were flown by the Hurricanes, A Flight was still non-operational and the pilots continued to work up on the Whirlwind.

Continuing delays in engine production meant that by October the squadron only had eight Whirlwinds on strength. In mock combats with the Hurricanes the Whirlwind proved to be superior in speed at low level and made the Hurricane look too slow. In November the Squadron gave up its Hurricanes and the Whirlwinds moved to Exeter. The Squadrons' first operational patrol was carried out on 3 December 1940 under the command of Squadron Leader Eeles. Eeles was posted to Drem on the 16th and Squadron Leader Munro took over as the new CO. In an effort to make some use of the new Whirlwinds one flight from No.263 Squadron was posted to St Eval on the Cornish coast.

During January 1941 the Squadron still maintained a detachment at St Eval. During Luftwaffe raids on South Wales and the South East of England E-Boats were stationed off the coast to act as rescue boats in case any enemy aircraft came down in the sea. It was decided to try and engage these boats as they returned to their French base. These were given the code name Chameleon. Three such patrols were carried out on 9th, 13th and 17th but no E-Boats were encountered.

The St Eval detachment carried out a number of scrambles to intercept enemy aircraft. Most were unsuccessful but on 12th Pilot Officer D.Stein caught a Ju88 40m South West of the Scillies. After his initial attack the Junkers was last seen in a spiral dive and was credited as a probable. The first success for the squadron came on 8th February. During a patrol an Arado Ar196A-4 was attacked and shot down by Pilot Officer K.A.G.Graham, P6969/HE-V. During this engagement Graham was also shot down and killed by the return fire from the rear gunner. The rest of the month was pret-

ty quiet with the bulk of operations being flown from the St-Eval detachment. At the end of the month it was decided to send the rest of the squadron to St Eval so the unit could now operate as a whole. Squadron Leader Munro was out and his place was taken over by Squadron Leader A.H.Donaldson, the brother of Squadron Leader J.W.Donaldson who commanded the Squadron in Norway. During a patrol off the Cornish coast on 1 March 1941 Pilot Officer P.G.Thornton-Brown damaged a Ju88. Pilot Officer Thornton-Brown was in action again on 5th. He and Pilot Officer Kitchener damaged another Ju88 off the Scillies Isles. The action wasn't all one sided however. On 11th Pilot Officer H.H.Kitchener was severely injured when he was hit by return fire from a Ju88 off the Cornish coast at 1710hrs. He crash-landed his damaged aircraft, P6985/HE-J, which was destroyed in the subsequent fire.

On 14 March 1941, the same day Pilot Officer P.G.Thornton-Brown crashed at Portreath while returning from a convoy patrol and seriously injured. On 18th the whole squadron moved to Portreath and for the remainder of the month the Squadron took part in numerous convoy patrols. On the first day of April Squadron Leader Donaldson (P6998), and Flight Lieutenant Crooks (P6989) intercepted a Do215 5m North of Preddannack and claimed it as damaged. Flight Lieutenant DA.C.Crooks failed to return and it was thought he was shot down by the rear gunner. Flying Officer B.Howe and Pilot Officer A.Tooth came across one He111s on 6th which was claimed as damaged. During 7th a lone raider was tracked near Falmouth. Flying Officer Ferdinand and Sergeant King were scrambled to intercept. They came across a Ju88 to the South of Falmouth and after a brief engagement it escaped into cloud, but with no result. Another move occurred in April, this time back to Filton.

Flying Officer B.Howe died on 20 April 1941 as a result of an accident near Wittering airfield. His Whirlwind, P6992 broke up in the air after a part became detached from the airframe. Another pilot was lost on 30th; Pilot Officer G.S.Milligan was

On 8 February 1941, while flying Whirlwind HE-V/P6969, Pilot Officer K.A.G.Graham claimed the first aerial victory by a Whirlwind. The victim was an Ar196 float plane. (*Phil Jarrett*)

undertaking mock attacks on a Wellington when his Whirlwind, P7008 broke up in the air and crashed. These two losses may have been the result of the wing leading edge slats breaking off during tight turns. Other similar incidents occurred and as a result a decision was taken to lock the slats in place. This had no detrimental effect on the aircraft's performance.

During 1941 Fighter Command started to carry out sweeps over occupied Europe. At first there were two types of sweeps, *Rhubarbs* and *Circuses*. A *Rhubarb* was carried out solely by fighters. A *Circus* was carried out by a small number of bombers with a large escort of fighters. The idea was to entice the Luftwaffe up into the air where the RAF fighters would be waiting for them. It was decided not to risk the Whirlwinds on these operations as they were thought to be too vulnerable, much in the same way as the Bf110s were, when operated over England. However it was decided to try them on *Warheads*, which were low level attacks on enemy airfields. The Whirlwinds were also to take part in *Mandolins*, which were unescorted fighter attacks on enemy airfields.

During May the Squadron was involved in 81 convoy patrols and

Lieutenant Hughes attacked Querqueville airfield. Both Whirlwinds were damaged during the attack. Flight Lieutenant T.P.Pugh and Pilot Officer D.W.Mason carried out an attack on Maupertus airfield. On the way home Mason attacked an E-Boat ¼ mile North of Cherbourg. It was left in a sinking condition, which Mason claimed as sunk. *Warhead* 3, another 2-part operation, was carried out the next day. Squadron Leader A.H.Donaldson and Sergeant Holmes attacked Maupertus airfield. Both pilots strafed Ju87s and Bf109s claiming one Ju87 destroyed with two more Ju87s and two Bf109s as damaged. Two lorries, one with troops in, were also shot up. The second patrol was a shipping recce of Cherbourg by Flight Lieutenant Hughes and Sergeant D.St.Jowitt. No shipping was seen but a wireless station was shot up.

The Squadron returned to Maupertus on 6 August with *Warhead* 5. Pilot Officer C.P.Rudland claimed one Ju87 destroyed on the ground and one Bf109 that was on its take off run. Two more Ju87s were claimed destroyed on the ground, while two more plus two Bf109s were claimed as damaged. On the run out over the coast two tankers were encountered and both of these were damaged.

C.P.Rudland's combat reports 06.08.41.

Claim No.1
I was Red 2 on Warhead operation No.5, the object of which was to attack Maupertus aerodrome. At about 1250 we came in over the aerodrome from the North at about 100 feet. I saw an ME109 just taking off. It had not left the ground, but it had got its tail up. I fired a two seconds burst at it from 50 yards, and it immediately burst into fames.
I claim 1 ME109 as destroyed.

Claim No.2
I was Red 2 on Warhead No.6. About 5 miles off the French coast we were met by three ME109E followed by 12/20 more. In the melee which followed I saw a Whirlwind coming towards me with one ME109 on its tail. I made a head on attack firing a 1.5 seconds burst, and I saw several of my shells strike just behind the cockpit. I broke away over the E/A, passing about 6 feet above it. I then did a steep turn to Port. I could see the Whirlwind but, no ME109. SL Howell of 118 Squadron which was arriving on the scene saw an ME1089 go into sea.
I claim 1 ME109 as destroyed
06.08.41 at 16.00 off the French coast, between Quarqueville an Cap de la Hague.

---

about a dozen scrambles. No enemy aircraft were encountered. The convoy patrols continued into June and during the month 67 patrols were carried out with a further 7 scrambles involving a total of 152 sorties. Two pilots were lost during the second week. Sergeant R.G. Pascoe on 11th and the next day after Pilot Officer R.F.Ferdinand, both being killed. The Squadron took part in their first offensive operation on 14th. *Warhead* 1 was a double sweep against Querqueville and Maupertus airfields. Squadron Leader Donaldson and Pilot Officer Rudland carried out the sweep against Querqueville. On the way out over the coast a lighthouse was also damaged. Squadron Leader Donaldson was hit in the port engine nacelle but he managed to get back to base safely. The second sweep was flown by Flight Lieutenant Pugh and Pilot Officer Mason against Maupertus airfield. Here the target was covered in mist and so the attack was cancelled. July was another quiet month for the squadron with convoy patrols being the norm.

The first week of August was a busy one for the Squadron. On 4th the Squadron carried out its second *Warhead* and again it was a double operation. Squadron Leader Donaldson and Flight

Later that same day *Warhead* 6 was put into motion. This was to locate and destroy the two tankers that were previously damaged in the earlier raid. Although the tankers were not found the four Whirlwinds encountered a number of Bf109s and a general dogfight took place. Pilot Officer Rudland claimed one of the Bf109s shot down, while another was claimed by Flight Sergeant R.A.Brackley. Squadron Leader A.H.Donaldson claimed a third as damaged. The Squadron also carried out the occasional escort mission. On 12th the Whirlwinds escorted 54 Blenheims on their way to Cologne during Operation 77, although the Whirlwinds only went as far as Antwerp. On the return journey the squadron attacked a number of vessels. One *flak* barge was sunk and another damaged.

Lannion airfield was the target on 24th. Newly promoted Wing Commander A.H.Donaldson led Flight Lieutenant P.T.Pugh, Pilot Officer C.P.Rudland and Sergeant A.V.Albertini on a sweep over the airfield. A RDF station and a navigation beacon were damaged. On the return flight nine Bf109s were spotted but they refused to enter combat.

nother 2-part operation took place on 26th. Maupertus airfield

Two Whirlwinds, HE-Z and HE-S, taking off from St Eval, in 1941, for another patrol. (*Chris Goss*).

was attacked and five Ju87s claimed destroyed on the ground. During an attack on Lannion airfield five Ju88s were claimed destroyed. *Mandolin* 3 was carried out against Lannion airfield on 29th. Flight Lieutenant J.G.Hughes and Sergeant J.W.E.Holmes damaged a RDF station and a blockhouse. On the last day of the month the squadron took part in *Gudgeon* 4 a cover for returning Blenheims that had attacked Lannion airfield. Twelve Whirlwinds took part in another Gudgeon operation on 4 September 1941. A formation of six Blenheims had raided Cherbourg Harbour when six Bf109s were encountered. In the dogfight that followed Sergeant Brackwell was shot down baled out off Cherbourg and was taken prisoner.

Blenheim escort was again the order of the day on 8th. A convoy had been sighted near Alderney and 11 Whirlwinds provided escort. As well as providing escort the Whirlwinds were to be used for *flak* suppression. The results were rather good with one 400t vessel left on fire, one tug sunk and two tugs and three barges damaged. Sergeant King had his aircraft damaged by a Bf109.

Early on the 10th two Whirlwinds set off to attack the Gestapo HQ at Quineville. Poor visibility hampered the mission and as they crossed the coast one of them, P7001 piloted by Pilot Officer Mason was hit by *flak* from a gun position and crashed. Flying Officer Stein then carried out four attacks on the gun position and silenced it.

Another *Mandolin* was laid on for Lannion airfield the next day. The attack in the late evening left one Ju88 destroyed and two dispersal pens damaged. As the formation neared Plymouth Sergeant T.Hunter, P7009 experienced problems and baled out 5 miles from the coast. His body was not recovered. Flying Officer H.Coghlan ran out of fuel and crashlanded during his approach to land at Predannack.

In September No.137 Squadron was being equipped with Whirlwinds and a large number of pilots and ground personnel were posted from the Squadron to No.137 Squadron.

With the posting of so many experienced pilots an influx of new pilots fresh from OTUs arrived during October. A period of intense training soon followed and as a result there was very little operational flying, apart from two missions at the end of the month. During a practise flight on 9th two Whirlwinds collided. Flight Lieutenant H.Coghlan was able to bale out but Pilot Officer OJ.H.Hoskins was killed.

An attack on the airfield at Morlaix was scheduled for the 29th. Two pilots, Flight Sergeant R.A.Brackley (P7651) and Sergeant C.P.King, (P7007) took off from Predannack at 1445hrs. They attacked from the south and Brackley claimed a Ju88 as damaged. King fired a burst at a hanger, which was observed to be hit; he then fired at a Ju88 but failed to notice any damage. King collided with a mast, which damaged his port coolant tank. As King headed for home he shot up a gun post on the way. Shutting down the overheated engine King was able to cross the coast and land back at base okay.

Another two-man strike was laid on for Morlaix again the next day. Flying Officer D.Stein (P7615) and Sergeant K.C.Ridley (P6994) took off at 0945hrs. The airfield defences were ready and Sergeant Ridley was hit by *flak* but managed to get back to base, although he ran off the runway. Flying Officer D.Stein was not so lucky and he failed to return. It was first thought he may have survived and taken captive but it was later learned that he had been killed.

During early November Flight Lieutenant Coghlan was promoted to Squadron Leader and posted to take command of No.137 Squadron. On 6 November 1941 *Rhubarb* 56 was carried out near the Cherbourg Peninsula. No shipping seen and the section set course back to base. Sergeant J.J.Robinson, P6970 appeared to dip one wing into the sea and crash. He was presumed killed.

Another Rhubarb took place the next day to recce distillery targets. The object was to locate various distilleries for future targets. A number of Bf109s were encountered and Sergeant King claimed one shot down. Flying Officer G.B.Warnes was attacked by two Bf109s but he was able to evade them by doing steep turns at sea level.

During early December a move was made from Filton to Charmy Down. Sergeant D.E.Prior was killed on 14th. He was participating in a search light co-operation exercise when his aircraft, P7044 was seen to crash near Coleford. The rest of the month was quiet with no encounters with the enemy.

A New Year of Combat

January 1942 was a very quiet month for the Squadron due to the bad weather, which curtailed most flying. In the middle of the month the Squadron moved to Colerne. Training in air-to-air firing and practise attacks both with and without camera guns were carried out whenever the weather permitted. On 5 January 1942 it was announced that all fighter Squadrons should become operational at night as well as during the day. Two days later Pilot Officer H.J.Blackshaw and Sergeant W.Lovell were scrambled after two 'bandits' (later identified as Bf109s) that were reported between Plymouth and Ibsley. One of these (Bf109E-7 W.Nr4970) suffered engine failure and the pilot, *Unteroffizier* Kurt Thüne from 1./(F)123 baled out and was captured near Bovey Tracey.

February brought another move for the Squadron, this time to Fairwood Common in Glamorganshire on 10th. On 12 February 1942 Squadron leader T.P. Pugh, DFC was posted from the squadron as Squadron Leader Tactics to HQ No.82 Group. His place was taken over by Squadron Leader R.S.Woodward, DFC who came from No.137 Squadron. The runways at Fairwood Common were not really suitable for the Whirlwinds and as a result a number of accidents occurred. On 13th Pilot Officer J.P.Coyne was injured after his Whirlwind, P7108 swung on landing and overturned. Between 19th and 21st problems also arose with the Peregrine engines, which resulted in a temporary grounding of all aircraft in late February. The defect was traced to faulty three way unions, which supply oil to the camshaft and supercharger bearings. Stronger unions were supplied by Westlands and fitted to all Whirlwinds.

The flying ban was lifted on 4th March and the training continued. Three days later on 7th Sergeant P.A.Jardine suffered a heavy landing. He hit the ground hard and burst both tyres, causing the Whirlwind, P7039 to overturn. Jardine survived the accident but suffered spinal injuries. Convoy patrols continued and on 25th the Whirlwind was presented to the press and public for the first time. The Whirlwind was no longer a secret.

Another Whirlwind was lost on 1st of April when Pilot Officer P.Harvey was coming into land. He was hit by a 50mph crosswind and bounced on landing. The Whirlwind, P7112 turned over and disintegrated. Harvey was able to walk away from the wreckage with little more than a bruised arm. The next day Sergeant D.Small suffered from hydraulic failure in P7041 and collided with a fuel bowser, although it has also been reported that Sergeant B.C.Abrams was the pilot and he hit a dispersal pen. On 18th April the squadron moved to Angle. Convoy patrols were still the norm. On 27th Flight Lieutenant C.P.Rudland was ordered up to shot down a loose barrage balloon. Although he only had ball ammunition the balloon went up in flames. On 30th a *Ramrod* was carried out to Morlaix airfield, although bad weather prevented the target from being attacked.

During May the Squadron was heavily committed to convoy patrols. The Squadron flew a total of 535 hours and 55 minutes on operational flights and 282 hours and 40 minutes of non-operational flights. No accidents of any kind were reported, surely a record for the Squadron if not Fighter Command. Several scrambles took place but no interceptions took place.

On 5 June 1942 the Squadron recommenced *Rhubarb* operations. Four Whirlwinds took off from Predannack at 1513hrs to attack Lannion airfield. Squadron Leader R.S.Woodward attacked a row of five Ju88s. As he completed his attacked he noticed that they looked like dummies. Pilot Officer J.P.Coyne also recognised the Ju88s as dummies after he had attacked them. Pilot Officer H.J.Blackshaw also saw the dummy Junkers and avoided them. He did however spot a Ju88 being serviced in a hanger and opened fire scoring a number of hits. Flight Sergeant H.D.Muirhead achieved hits on two blister hangers in the northern part of the airfield.

A well known photograph, taken in 1942, of P7116 "Bellows Argentina No. 2" which was Squadron Leader P.T.Pugh's personal aircraft at the end of his posting to the squadron. Squadron Leader Thomas Pugh carried out only two operational flights in this machine before it was passed to Robert S.Woodward No.263 Squadron's new Commanding Officer. In all P7116 accumulated 49.4 flying hours in 40 operational sorties.
The exact number of Whirlwinds christened "Bellows", which were funded by the Fellowship of the Bellows (Argentina or Uruguay), is uncertain. (*Phil Jarrett*).

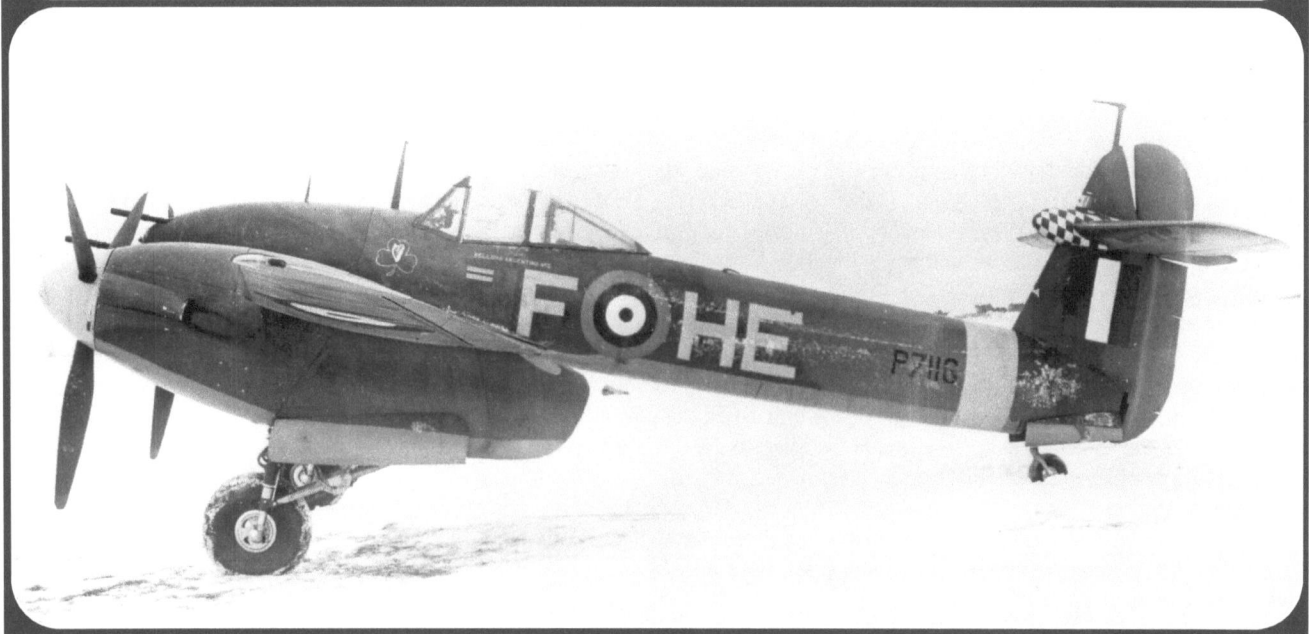

Enter the Whirli-Bomber

Plans were in hand to equip the Whirlwinds with bombs. Trials were carried out in July 1942 when one aircraft was fitted with two MkIII universal bomb racks outboard of the engine nacelles. At first 250-lb bombs were fitted but later 500-lb were tested. The 500-lb bombs put a strain on the wings and so only 250-lb bombs were to be used. A simple push button release was fitted near the throttle levers. A jettison switch was also fitted. These modified aircraft became known as Whirlibombers. During a dive these bomb-laden aircraft had a tendency to drop the port wing, plus pilots were advised to drop both bombs at once. If they dropped them singly then it was advised to drop the port one first.

Although still based at Angle, B Flight was detached to Portreath from 1 to 8 July 1942. Convoy patrols and scrambles were the routine for the squadron. It wasn't until the end of the month that they saw any real action.

At 1534hrs on 23rd Squadron Leader R.S.Woodward led twelve Whirlwinds from their advance based at Predannack. As they approached the Lizard at 300ft they met up with their escort from No.234 Squadron. Squadron Leader Woodward P6990 and Pilot Officer Coyne P7062 attacked railway trucks at Landivisiau Station. They then flew back to Predannack via Morlaix where they shot up some trucks. As they crossed the Channel Coyne attacked two vessels and saw strikes on one of them. Here they joined up with four other Whirlwinds and set course for home. They spotted one Whirlwind being followed by two Bf109s. Before they could intervene the Whirlwind was shot down. As they neared the coast they saw another Whirlwind being pursued by three more Bf109s. Although Woodward turned back he did not see the aircraft again. Flight Sergeant C.P.King (P7057) and Pilot Officer V.L.Currie (P7035) attacked a truck near Morlaix. Pilot Officer Curries was last seen with four other Whirlwinds near the French coast. It may

have been Currie that was shot down over the sea by the Bf109s.

Pilot Officer J.J.Walker (P7060) and Sergeant B.C.Abrams (P7120) flew south to Landivisiau and turned towards St Tregonnec. A train was attacked in Belair Station and hits were registered. Pilot Officer Walker failed to return. Flight Lieutenant G.B.Warnes (P7117) and Pilot Officer S.Lovell (P7007) attacked a number of targets to the north of a railway line between Landivisiau and Landerneau. Pilot Officer J.W.E.Holmes (P7056) and Sergeant W.R.Wright (P7090) attacked the same targets as Green Section plus the same target that was attacked by White Section. Flight Lieutenant C.P.Rudland (P7014) and Pilot Officer P.Harvey (P6979) fired on three railway trucks coming out of St Pol de Leon. One truck was left glowing red.

On 18 August 1942 the Squadron moved from Angle to Colerne. There was very little in the way of flying during the month. The maintenance crews worked very hard at fitting all aircraft with bomb racks and by the end of the month this had been completed. A number of enemy shipping was reported in the Channel Islands area on 4th. As the Squadron was the only operational fighter-bomber Squadron within No.10 Group four of the Whirlwinds were sent to RAF Bolt Head. From here they carried out two *Roadstead* operations in the Channel Islands area but failed to find any enemy shipping.

Eight Whirlwinds led by Squadron Leader R.S.Woodward took off on an anti shipping strike in the Alderney - Cap de la Hague area on 10th. Four large armed trawlers were found and in the resulting attack two of them were claimed sunk. These ships involved were the coasters *Henca* (305t) and *Tinda* (280t) escorted by VP207 and VP209 of the 2.*Verpostenflotille*. During the attack the *Henca* was hit by one bomb, causing it to capsize and sink in seven minutes. VP207 was hit and damaged, with two crew killed and seventeen injured. Three days later the rest

Whirlwind P6691/HE-R on a dispersal in March 1942. This Whirlwind spent two years with No.263 Squadron and was repaired twice, in March and July 1942, before it was struck off charge after another mishap on 9 February 1943. (*Phil Jarrett*)

Another view of three No.263 Squadron Whirlwinds believed to be at Angle in the summer of 1942. *(ww2images)*

of the Squadron moved to Warmwell. To help relieve other squadrons or when RAF Zeal was non-operational the Whirlwinds undertook other types of sorties including Air Sea Rescue flights off the Channel Islands. On 21 September 1942 Sergeant P.A.Jardine was lost when his Whirlwind, P7003 dived into the ground near Dorset. Night flying practise was carried out on the night of 23rd-24th. It was hoped that as many pilots as possible would be operational at night in order to carry out night operations. The rest of the month was pretty quiet and although number of operations took place nothing of importance was noted.

On 7 November 1942 Pilot Officer D.R.Gill led four Whirlwinds on a *Rhubarb*. After bombing a railway line Gill, P7043 disappeared and failed to return. It is thought he may have been shot down by *flak*. Pilot Officer E.Brearley and Sergeant F.W.Yates carried out a successful *Rhubarb* on 16th. A number of railway lines were destroyed and on the return journey Sergeant Yates attacked and damaged an E-Boat. The remainder of the month continued with *Rhubards*, *Roadsteads* and shipping recce's but very little was encountered either due to a lack of targets or poor weather.

On 7 December 1942 a number of Whirlwinds took part in an anti-shipping strike to the Channel Islands. A small force of German ships, were spotted 10km to the South of Jersey. Coming into attack Warrant Officer D.B.McPhail was hit by a hail of AA fire from one of the ships and Whirlwind P6987 crashed into the sea. Squadron Leader R.S.Woodward, P7105 was also shot down and killed. Four of the ships were claimed as sunk or seriously damaged. One of these ships may have been the *Kronwijk* (622t), which was lost off Jersey on this day.

The next day Flight Lieutenant G.B.Warnes was promoted to Squadron Leader and posted to command the Squadron. In the afternoon of 14th two Whirlwinds flown by J.P.Coyne (P7057) and M.T.Cotton (P7052) carried out a sweep to the North of Barfluer. They failed to spot any suitable targets and set course for home. They were roughly 30km North of Cherbourg when they met and engaged two FW190s from 10./JG2, which were returning from a raid on Swanage. Both Coyne and Cotton fired at the FW190s but could only claim one as damaged. Both Whirlwinds returned undamaged but dangerously low on fuel. Flying for the remainder of the year consisted of practise flying, shooting and bombing.

1943 : LAST YEAR FOR THE WHIRLWIND

The start of the New Year was very quiet for the Squadron. Although numerous convoy patrols and *Rhubarbs* were carried out no major successes were reported.

On 12 February 1943 Flying Officer P.Harvey, (P7094) and Sergeant D.J.Williams (P7052) took from Warmwell for a *Rhubarb*. They crossed the coast near Cap de Carteret and just inland the spotted two goods trains. Harvey attacked one and saw strikes form his cannon hit the engine. Williams may have attacked the other train but his Whirlwind, P7052 was hit by *flak* and headed for the coast. As he crossed the coast he sank lower towards the water until he eventually crashed into the sea 4m off Cap de Caterat. Harvey circled the area and saw Williams in the water trying to get into his dinghy. After a couple of orbits he headed for home. As soon as he landed he was off again to lead an air sea rescue Walrus from No.276 Squadron to pick up Williams. When they reached the area the sea was too rough for the Walrus to land so reluctantly he set course back to base.

An Army co-operation exercise was held on 19 February 1943. Whirlwinds carried out a number of dummy attacks on army transport to give them an idea of what it was like to be attacked from the air. During one such attack Flight Sergeant F.L.Hicks hit a tree and his Whirlwind, P7062 cartwheeled into the ground and exploded, killing the pilot. During early March, A Flight and the Squadron HQ was based at Harrowbeer, while B Flight was at Fairwood Common. The early part of the month was taken up with convoy patrols and the occasional dusk patrol.

Roadstead operations were the main course for the first two

In autumn 1942 No.263 Squadron moved to Warmwell and joined No.10 Group. The Whirlwind was now being used as a fighter-bomber and this one is armed with 250-lb bombs under the wings. (*Chris Goss*).

weeks in April, although very little in the way of targets was found. On 14th during *Roadstead* 52 to the West of Brest Sergeant MacAuley, P7010 failed to return. Two days later, during a night *Rhubarb* on 16-17th Flying Officer E.Brearley (P6095) was lost in the Isigney area. His body was later washed ashore at Swanage. The Squadron suffered a heavy blow on another night sortie during 17-18th. During a shipping recce from the Channel Islands to Caen Flying Officer P.Harvey (P7090) and Flying Officer C.P. King (P7117) failed to return. During a later shipping recce to Cabourg Flying Officer B.C.Abrams (P7099) also failed to return.

The Squadron exacted some revenge on 27th. Squadron Leader G.B.Warnes (P7113) led six Whirlwinds on a shipping recce just South of Jersey. Here they spotted a convoy of nine ships. A barge was probably sunk and one ship estimated at 1,500t was set on fire plus an armed trawler was seriously damaged. Two other ships, including an E-Boat were shot up. No Whirlwinds were lost during this operation.

Another convoy was located and attacked the next day. Pilot Officer M.T.Cotton received a *flak* hit to his starboard wing but he returned to base with out any further mishap. This convoy was subject to another attack the following day. One of the escort vessels was sunk during this attack.

After this short period of intense operations the number of serviceable Whirlwinds had dropped to a low level. It was getting rather difficult to replace the losses, as no aircraft were available from either Westlands or the Maintenance Units that provided back up aircraft. Also the number of qualified pilots to fly the night sorties was well below the required number to maintain the squadron at an operational level. Therefore the squadron was put on a 30-minute readiness level.

As with previous months the first couple of weeks of May were without any major success. This changed on 15 May 1943, although it also saw the loss of a pilot. During a night shipping recce Flying Officer A.Lee-White (P7059) bombed a 2,500t ship and saw a large explosion. Later Squadron Leader G.B.Warnes, H.J.Blackshaw, J.W.E.Holmes and J.I.Simpson attacked a convoy at Barfleur. During the return flight Blackshaw was seen to orbit Exeter and Harrowbeer. His aircraft then dived into the ground and exploded, killing the pilot. During a shipping recce carried out the next day two Fw190s were engaged by the Whirlwinds. Flying Officer Lee-White and Coyne managed to obtain strikes on both enemy aircraft but they broke off and escaped any further damage. The Whirlwinds still carried their two 250lb during this engagement.

A large convoy action took place on the night of 21-22nd. Squadron Leader G.B.Warnes (P7113) led four other pilots to an area between Cap de la Hague and Cherbourg. Warnes bombed a 3,500t vessel and stayed near the convoy to direct the attacks of the other pilots. Holmes (P7040) and Cotton (P7108) bombed the same vessel as Warnes. Coyne (P7007) bombed and sank one of the escorting trawlers. As Flying Officer Lee-White (P7059) came into attack his starboard engine was hit by *flak* and it burst into flames. He continued his attack on one of the trawlers. As he prepared to bale out the flames died down and he decided to head back to base. The engine started to burn again but he landed back at Warmwell safely.

The 23rd saw four Whirlwinds, Pilot Officers Holmes (P7040), Ridley (P7000), Coyne (P6974) and Cotton (P7089), take off for an anti-shipping strike near Guernsey. The fighter-bombers had an escort of Spitfires from the Ibsley Wing. On coming through the Russel Strait they spotted a line of seven ships near St Peters Port. Coming in on a North-South run the pilots braved the murderous flak that was thrown up from the ships.

As the pilots dropped their bombs they were unable to observe much damage due to the intense *flak*, although the bombs dropped by Pilot Officer Holmes were seen to explode on the mid-section of one coaster. It was later reported that the ship, an ex-Dutch coaster *Oost Vlaanderen*, 421t sank. In return Cotton's Whirlwind was hit by accurate 20mm *flak* and holed in the starboard wing fuel tank. On return the aircraft was inspected and subsequently struck off charge as being unrepairable. Again the number of serviceable aircraft in the squadron was giving cause for concern. On 29 May 1943 it was announced that No.137 Squadron was being re-equipped with Hurricanes. Their Whirlwinds were transferred to No.263 Squadron, which brought their serviceable number up to around 20. A number of No.137 Squadron pilots were also posted into the squadron.

On 15 June 1943 Pilot Officer Cotton (P7000) was shot down by *flak* after dropping his bombs on a minesweeper. During this attack on a convoy to the North East of Sark an M Class minesweeper, M483 was sunk, possibly by Flying Officer A.Lee-White (P7097). Flight Sergeant G.A.Wood's Whirlwind, P7110 was also hit by *flak* in the tail and rudder.The day also saw the arrival of Squadron Leader E.R.Baker DFC to take over command of the Squadron. Due to an increased influx of new pilots the Squadron moved to Zeals, Wiltshire for a period of intensive training. By this time the squadron was down to just 10 serviceable aircraft.

On 12 July 1943 the Squadron moved back to Warmwell, Dorset to begin operations across the Channel. During 13th Sergeant L.J.Knott was coming in to land when he stalled from 50-80ft and crashed short of the airfield. The Whirlwind, P7110 was destroyed but Knott was safe. Four recce patrols were carried out on 13th, 18th, 20th and 23rd but no major action was encountered, other than *flak*. The rest of July was very quiet. On 1 August 1943 Sergeant C.P.Cooper bounced P6981 on landing and crashed. Cooper was slightly injured but the Whirlwind was a write off.

Geoffrey B. Warnes was unique in at least two ways. First he was short sighted but was allowed to fly wearing contact lenses and secondly because he became the only Whirlwind pilot to be awarded the DSO, in July 1943, while commanding No.263 Squadron. He served with No.263 Squadron for two tours, September 1941 - June 1943 and from December 1943 until he was killed in action on 22 February 1944. He led the Squadron twice from December 1942 onwards and for his second tour.

During 11th a strike was laid on after a number of E-Boats were reported in the estuary of Abervrach. Squadron Leader Baker (P7115) led six other Whirlwinds on the strike. An escort was provided by Spitfires from No.302 (Polish) Squadron, which were to provide *flak* suppression. Coming in at low-level the Spitfires went in first. As the Whirlwinds came in they selected their targets and dropped their bombs. Squadron Leader Bakers

Whirlwind P7059 starting to taxi out for another flight. As it was not loaded with bombs it was probably a training flight. (*Chris Goss*).

Whirlwind P7059 starting to taxi out for another flight. As it was not loaded with bombs it was probably a training flight.
(*Chris Goss*).

bombs were seen to hit one E-boat, which blew up. Altogether four E-boats and one trawler were claimed to have blown up from direct hits, while one E-boat was left in flames. *Flak* was reported as very light from the E-Boats but heavy from the shore. The only damage to the Whirlwinds was one bullet in the engine nacelle of one fighter.

The E-boats that were attacked were from the 4th and 5th E-boat Flotillas. The War Diary for the unit states that on 11 August 1943 20-25 fighters and fighter-bombers attacked E-Boats moored in l'Abervrach. E-boat S-121 was hit by bombs and set on fire. The ammunition then exploded and the E-Boat sank. Two other E-Boats, S-84 and S-136 received damage to their hulls and engines due to machine guns, cannons and bomb splinters. They were out of action for two weeks while undergoing repairs. S-117, possibly from the 4th Flotilla was also heavily damaged.

Squadron Leader E.R.Baker carried out a night recce of the Channel Islands on 14th. He came across a lone E-Boat and dropped his bombs on it causing an explosion. A little later, while of Guernsey he came across a He111 and shot this down into the sea.

The next night the squadron undertook a recce over Cherbourg harbour. Squadron Leader E.R.Barker dropped his bombs on an armed trawler, which was last seen in a sinking condition. This may have been the ex-Dutch *Iris* of 200t, which was sunk at Cherbourg by aircraft on 15 August 1943.

OPERATION *STARKEY*

Operation *Starkey* took place between 16 August and 9 September 1943. It was basically a ruse to lure the Germans into believing the Allies were going to invade France near Boulogne. It was also intended to divert valuable German resources from the Eastern Front. The operation involved mainly British and Canadian forces with the added help from the United States Army Air Force. The British Second Army was deployed to the Dover, Folkstone and Newhaven area while the Canadian First Army moved into the Portsmouth and

Southampton area. The operation was split into three phases; the Preliminary Phase 16 to 24 August, Preparatory Phase 25 August to 7 September and the Culminating Phase 8 to 9 September. The role of the air forces was to bomb nearby airfields, railways, industrial and other targets of opportunity.

The Whirlwinds of No.263 Squadron took part in two operations on the 8 and 9 September. For these operations the Squadron moved to Manston airfield and came under the command of No.11 Group. Aircraft that took part in this operation were given black and white stripes on the wings. Twin-engine aircraft also had their noses painted white. This applied to the Whirlwinds.

Operation *Chattanooga Choochoo* commenced on 17th September. This operation was devised by Squadron Leader Baker in co-operation with No.10 Group Intelligence. The aim of the operation was to sever the main Rennes-Brest railway line between Lamballe and Morlaix. If the railway could be severed then the stranded trains should be easy targets for the roving Whirlwinds and Mosquitoes. During a strike on Morlaix airfield on 23rd Flight Sergeant G.Wood was shot down in P7113. He managed to evade capture and returned to the UK with help from the Resistance.

During the early evening of 8th October Squadron Leader E.R.Baker (P7102) successfully bombed an E-Boat off Varriville. He landed back at base at 2025hrs. Two hours later two pilots landed back and reported that they had shot up a 2,500t flak ship. Immediately Squadron Leader Baker organised a strike on the ship. On arrival in the target area the ship was located and attacked. *Flak* was very heavy from Alderney and Cap de la Hague as well as the flak-ship. A sea haze was also making it difficult to locate the target and there was an increased risk of collision. Squadron Leader Baker ordered the formation to return to base. On their return they were informed that Warmwell was covered in fog and to land at Tangmere. Pilot Officer Simpson (P7047) suffered engine failure and as he came in to land at Tangmere the other engine failed as well. He crashed 100 yards short of the runway and was killed when he hit an anti-landing post.

These train busting sorties continued. Two trains were damaged by Pilot Officer H.M.Proctor (P6979) and Flight Sergeant I.D.Dunlop (P7055) on 19th. In the afternoon of the same day Pilot Officer N.P.Blacklock (P6971) and Sergeant Beaumont (P7046) hit a goods train near Airel. On landing back at base Pilot Officer Blacklock overshot and in order to prevent a major crash, raised the landing gear and bellied in.

During the 24th Flight Sergeant L.S.Gray (P6986) was shot down and captured. Flying Officer P.T.R.Mercer's aircraft (P6979) was hit by *flak* twice and he crashed into the sea. Flight Lieutenant D.G.Ross (P6974) was hit in the starboard wing and he carried out a belly landing at Warmwell. The Whirlwind was later struck off charge. Flight Sergeant P.F.Cooper had taken hits to his undercarriage causing it to collapse on landing. Squadron Leader Baker was slightly injured by flying perspex when his canopy took a number of hits. All the remaining Whirlwinds were damaged by *flak*.

On 10 November 1943, a shipping strike near Guernsey found three ships, which were attacked. A small coaster and two escorting tugs were damaged. That same evening Flying Officer D.W.Sturgeon (P7012) carried out a night shipping recce. While South East of Sark he sighted four-five ships. He attacked but no results were seen. A second strike was laid on to attack the same ships. Squadron Leader Bakers bombs exploded alongside a trawler. The following night Flying Officers R.B.Tuff (P6997) and J.B.Holman (P7012) were to the West of Guernsey when Flying Officer Tuff sighted two tugs. He attacked and achieved a near miss. Bad weather prevented a number of sorties during the remainder of November, although the Munsterland was attacked on two further occasions on 25th and 26th.

By the beginning of December 263 Squadron started to receive Typhoons to replace their Whirlwinds making an end to the career of the Whirlwind.

When No.137 Squadron was formed on Whirlwinds in September 1941 it was command by Squadron Leader John Sample, an experienced pilot. He was a pre-war Auxiliary Air Force officer who had served in France with No.607 Squadron in 1940 before taking command of No.504 Squadron. He was awarded the DFC in June 1940 for service in the Battle of France, however his posting with No.137 Squadron was brief as he was killed in a flying accident on 28 October 1941. (*Andrew Thomas*).

No.137 Squadron
code : SF
September 1941 - June 1943

After a brief three-month existence in 1918 (when it had been formed to become a DH9-equipped bomber unit) No.137 Squadron was scheduled to be re-form at Colerne, in No.10 Group Fighter Command, on 20 September 1941. It was to become the second

Whirlwinds of No.137 Squadron lined up along the perimeter track at Matlask early in 1942. The nearest aircraft, SF-P, P6982, has earlier served with No.263 squadron; after accidental damage on 26 May 1942 it was repaired and stored at No.18 MU and scapped in September 1944. (*Chris Thomas*)

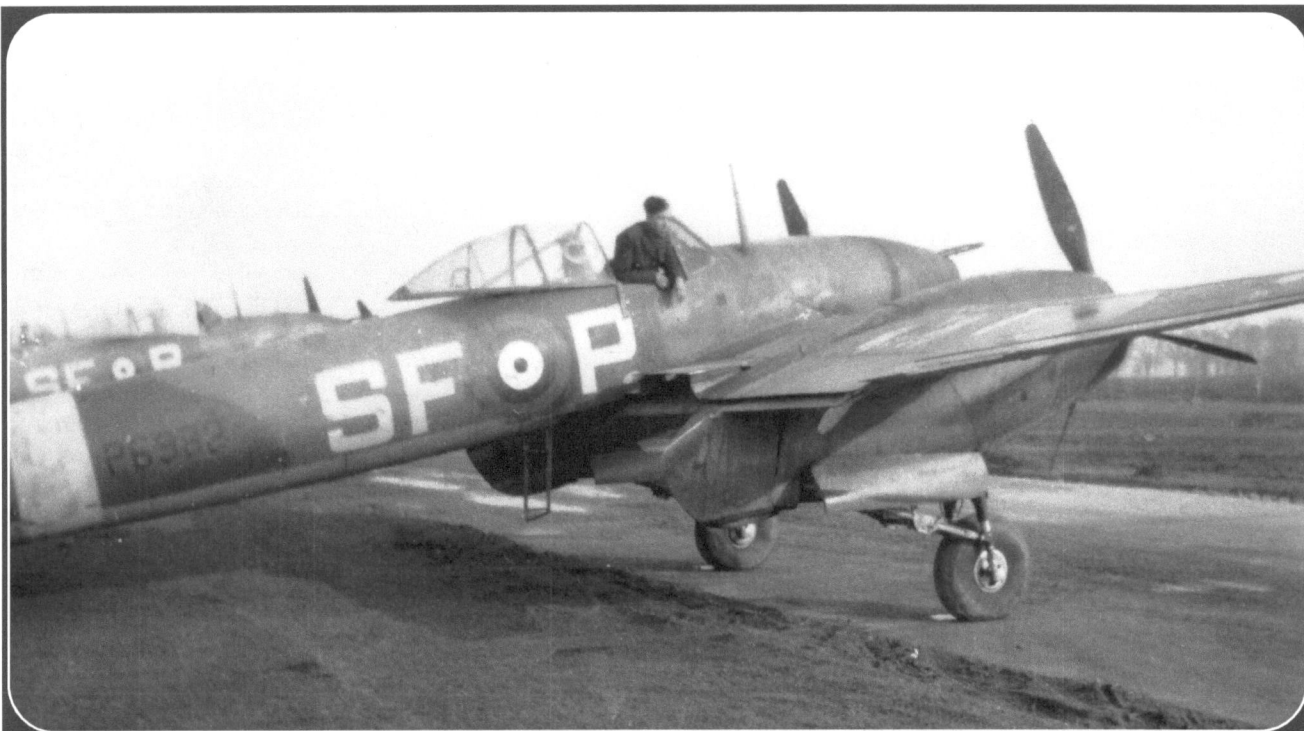

Whirlwind P6982/SF-P, taken from another angle. Because of the limited number of aircraft available, only two combat unit used the Whirlwind in operations. *(Chris Thomas)*

squadron to be fully equipped with the Westland Whirlwind. However, as it was due to replace No.125 Squadron (Beaufighter VI), then based at Colerne's satellite, Charmy Down, this latter station became No.137 Squadron's birthplace.

By the end of September the new unit had 18 Whirlwinds on charge, but only three pilots; more were posted in, mainly from the first Whirlwind unit, No.263 Squadron, so that by 19 October 1941, No.137 Squadron was able to field one operational Flight. The commanding officer, Squadron Leader J.Sample, DFC, had to convert to Whirlwinds, having flown Gladiators with No.607 Squadron before commanding No.504 Squadron, equipped with Hurricanes, throughout the Battle of Britain. Sample carried out the new unit's first operational sortie along with the South African Flying Officer C.A.G.Clark, flying to Predannack to undertake an attack on fuel containers which had been reported in railway sidings at Landerneau, inland from Brest. On arrival it was apparent that the fuel containers had been moved so the pilots attacked coal trucks and a locomotive.

CHAOTIC DEBUT

After this tentative start to operations the Squadron received a most unfortunate setback when, during practice interceptions, Squadron Leader Sample's Whirlwind was in collision with another Whirlwind flown by a new pilot. Sample's aircraft lost its tail unit and he spun to his death, although the trainee landed safely. Just two days later Flying Officer Clark, one of the Flight commanders and Sample's companion on the first operation, was forced to ditch in the Channel returning from another attack on Landerneau; although picked up by a destroyer, he died of his injuries. The Squadron was now declared non-operational, receiving 11 new pilots, all but one straight from No.56 OTU with no twin-engined experience (an Oxford was duly allocated to the Squadron to provide the requisite training). On 8 November the Squadron moved to the east coast (RAF Coltishall) undertaking

training flights and convoy patrols when the weather permitted. At the beginning of December 1941 the Squadron left the comfort of Coltishall for its less luxurious satellite, Matlask, which had been built the previous year. No.137 Squadron's first contact with the Luftwaffe came on 3 January 1942 when a Ju88 was intercepted 30 miles off Cromer but, in what was to become an all too familiar scenario, the enemy aircraft escaped into cloud. Interceptions of reconnaissance Do217s took place on 1st and 5th February and although these aircraft were attacked they escaped with no results observed.

The run of bad luck continued on 12 February 1942 when four Whirlwinds took off to carry out a convoy patrol but were unable to locate the Allied ships. However, two battleships were sighted and, believing them to be friendly, the Whirlwind pilots investigated; it was a fatal error. The ships were no less than the *Scharnhorst* and *Gneisnau* making their famous "Channel dash", with five or six destroyers and *flak* ships, and the Whirlwinds were immediately set upon by the Luftwaffe escort of 20 Bf109s. In the ensuing chaotic combat Pilot Officer J.L.DeHoux (RCAF) expended all his ammunition without apparent result and Canadian Flight Sergeant C.E.Mercer's guns frustratingly jammed with an enemy aircraft in his sights; although these two pilots returned safely Pilot Officer R.O.G.Häggberg, a Swede and Warrant Officer B.L.Robertson were not seen again. Two further pilots who took off to carry out the same patrol some 30 minutes after the first formation, also failed to return. All four were apparently shot down by the Bf109s.

March and April 1942 passed with fruitless Scrambles to investigate suspected "tracks", and uneventful convoy patrols. On 8 May 1942 six aircraft were detached to Coltishall operate at night against an expected raid on Norwich. A Do217 was seen but the Whirlwind pilot was not in position to attack. On 15 May 1942 however, Flight Sergeants J.R.Brennan and A.G.Brunet, both Canadians, intercepted a Ju88 and the former pilot claimed strikes before the Ju88 disappeared into cloud. His aircraft was hit by return fire and landed at Coltishall on one engine.

It seemed No.137 Squadron's luck had changed on 27 May 1942 when Brennan and Pilot Officer P.M.La Gette reported intercepting a Ju88 which, after attacks from both pilots, crashed in the sea 20 miles off Cromer. However, a Coastal Command Blenheim was last plotted at the same location and it is likely this was the "Ju88". Brennan was last seen heading east after the combat , reporting "everything under control" but was not seen alive again.

Another frustrating combat took place on 20 June 1942 when Warrant Officer C.E.Mercer and Flight Sergeant J.H.Ashton (both RCAF) were scrambled in the evening and sighted a Do217 crossing their path 2,000 yards ahead, some 30 or 40 miles east of Great Yarmouth. The Do217 dived to sea level and the Whirlwinds gave chase. Ashton made two attacks and Mercer expended all his ammunition, noting at least 3 or 4 strikes, but the Dornier made good its escape.

THE FIRST CONFIRMED VICTORY

July 1942 seemed to be going the same way when on the 6th another Ju88 escaped, albeit damaged, but the 25th of the month saw No.137 Squadron's first confirmed victory.

Two Whirlwinds were patrolling a convoy off Smiths Knoll in the early evening, Warrant Officer R.L.Smith spotted an unidentified aircraft approaching at sea level. As the aircraft, a mile distant and identified as a Ju88, turned away, the Whirlwinds gave chase and, with the advantage of height and a shallow dive, quickly closed to firing range. In fact the lead Whirlwind flown by Canadian Pilot Officer J.E.McClure overshot and as he turned away to reposition fire from the Ju88's dorsal turret hit the Whirlwind's starboard engine. Smith was positioned astern and having missed with his first burst from 500 yards, closed to 250 yards expending all his ammunition, seeing strikes on the starboard engine. Throttling back, McClure came in again from

astern and slightly starboard, opening fire with a 2-second burst at 100 yards, closing to 50 yards. At that range the effect of the Whirlwind's four closely-grouped 20mm cannon must have been devastating and as McClure broke away he saw flames from the fuselage and more strikes on the starboard engine. The Ju88 started to climb but McClure closed in again with a four-second burst closing to 25 yards. The Ju88 stalled and dived straight into the sea.

It seemed now that No.137 Squadron had the bit well and truly between its teeth, as the very next day two Ju88s and Do217 were intercepted during three separate sorties, but the Ju88s employed their low-level performance to escape and the Dornier, attacked at night, evaded whilst the Whirlwind pilot, Sergeant F.G.Waldron, was blinded by cannon flash. However, on the 29th of the same month another Ju88 fell to Squadron's guns when Flight Sergeant J.R.Rebbetoy (RCAF), and Sergeant H.L.O'Neill were vectored from their evening convoy patrol to intercept the hostile aircraft. In heavy mist, the Ju88 was not seen until it was 200 yards away, giving the German pilot no time to evade. Both pilots expended all their ammunition in several attacks but the Junkers flew on for another 15 miles before its bombs were jettisoned and it crashed into the sea with starboard wing ablaze.

At the beginning of August the Squadron flew to Drem, east of Edinburgh to take part in an Army exercise *Dryshod*. The units role was taken over temporarily by No.266 Squadron who flew their Hawker Typhoons into Matlask from Duxford. Two days before No.137 Squadron returned, No.266 Squadron demonstrated the new fighter's low-level performance by catching and destroying one of the elusive Ju88s, the first Typhoon victory.

A brief flurry of interceptions in mid August, which resulted in a Do217 destroyed and three further Ju88s damaged brought to an end this chapter of Squadron's history, as on 24 August 1942 the Squadron moved inland to Snailwell, north-east of Cambridge, where, it was informed its main duties would be night flying. Accordingly most of September was spent on night-

Whirlwind P7055 served with No.137 Squadron between November 1941 and February 1943. It was issued to No.263 Squadron in June 1943 and ended its career with this unit. By November 1943 it was one of the last operational Whirlwinds still in service. (*Chris Thomas*)

flying training and from 12th of the month, bombing practice, as the Whirlwinds were now being equipped to carry a 250- or 500-lb bomb under each wing. The only operation flown was a *Rodeo* on 3 September 1942 in which No.137 Squadron were escorted by 24 Spitfires from Nos.411 (RCAF) and 485 (NZ) Squadrons and 36 Typhoons of the Duxford Wing (Nos.56, 266 and 609 Squadrons). This impressive force swept over Belgium to Diximude but no enemy reaction was forthcoming. The Squadron moved to Manston, the nearest base to Occupied Europe on 17 September 1942, a move which promised rather more contact with the enemy. The rest of the month, however, was spent in more bombing and night flying practice.

Operations started again in October, with local patrols and shipping reccos. This was the period when Luftwaffe fighter-bomber attacks on the south coast intensified and on 25 October 1942 the new A Flight commander, Flight Lieutenant J.W.E.Holmes and Sergeant H.L.O'Neill attempted to intercept four Fw190s, but were unable to close or prevent them bombing Dungeness. Three days later Air Marshal Leigh-Mallory visited to brief the Squadron on its role at Manston; night-flying seemed to be forgotten and No.137 Squadron would be used on *Rhubarbs* and similar operations. These began disastrously on 31 October when three of four Whirlwinds that set out for Le Touquet failed to return. All fell victim to *flak* with one pilot taken prisoner and two in the Channel, only one of whom was rescued. In the afternoon of the same day six Whirlwinds intercepted a FW190 near Margate but, as if to emphasise the harsh environment in which they were now operating, despite the Whirlwinds 'clocking' 300 mph, the German fighter pulled away with ease.

During November the night flying practice was put to good use when Intruder sorties were added to No.137 Sqaudron's repetoire, the main targets being the railway systems. The location of the airfield meant engagements with the Luftwaffe could happen any time and on 19 December 1942 Flying Officer J.M.Bryan and Pilot Officer J.R.Rebbetoy (RCAF) on practice 'cloud flying' sighted two Fw190s

which they promptly attacked; after a dogfight in which both Whirlwind pilots got in bursts, the Fw190s turned for home, one streaming black smoke was last seen diving on its side from about 400 feet. The No.137 Squadron pilots were credited with a pro-bable.

FIRST AWARDS

At the end of January 1943 the first decoration received by a pilot of the Squadron was awarded, a DFC to Pilot Officer R.L.Smith (who already had a DFM) for his work on Blenheims before joining No.137 Squadron and for destroying (with McClure) a Ju88 and attacking four FW190 single-handed, as well as undertaking a number of successful Rhubarbs. The Squadron was now flying a mix of shipping patrols, *Rhubarbs* and *Intruders*, with mounting success. By 6 February 1943, Flying Officer Bryan had attacked and damaged 12 trains; ten days later he would be promoted to command A Flight. On 10 February 1943 Pilot Officer E.L.Musgrave (RAAF) attacked a 5000-ton motor vessel at night, off Boulogne; despite accurate defensive fire he dropped two 250 lb bombs which must have hit home as the vessel stopped for more than an hour and then took shelter in Boulogne Harbour. His aircraft was hit in the elevator and shrapnel pierced the canopy but he returned safely.

The 18 February 1943 brought a record 16 sorties in a night but with terrible price. Two pilots were lost when a Whirlwind taking-off collided with another taxying and bombs exploded. The 5 March 1943 brought a visit from the press in which Flight Lieutenant Bryan performed the required "beat-up" in SF-A. A week later he received a DFC for work with the Squadron, his score now stood at a Do217 destroyed, a FW190 probably destroyed and 20 trains damaged. On 14 March 1943 six Whirlwinds attacked Abbeville with 250-lb bombs, escorted by Spitfires of Nos.350 (Belgian) and 453 (RAAF) Squadrons as close cover and Nos.64 and 122 Squadrons as top cover. Bomb bursts were seen on NE side of aerodrome. At the end of the

P7037/SF-J ended its career with No.137 Squadron after this accident in October 1942. The pilot, D.A. Roberts (RNZAF) escaped uninjured and after repairs it was delivered to No.263 Squadron. *(D.A. Roberts via Paul Sortehaug)*

Whirlwind pilots of No.137 Sqn photographed at Manston on 5 March 1943. Left to right, Flying Officer R.L.Smith DFC, DFM, Flying officer E.L.Musgrave (RAAF) DFC, Pilot Officer D.A.Roberts, Sergeant J.M.Barclay, Warrant Officer A.G.Brunet (RCAF), Flight Lieutenant J.M.Bryan, Flying Officer J.L.Dehoux (RCAF), Sergeant A.C.Smith, Flying Officer A.C.McClure, Pilot Officer N.Dugdale, Sergeant T.A.Sutherland, Sergeant E.A.Bolster, Flying Officer J.M.Hadow, Squadron Leader H.StJ.Coghlan DFC, Flight Sergeant H.L.O'Neill, Flight Sergeant R.Woodhouse. (*Chris Thomas*).

month the Squadron carried out satisfactory trials with 500-lb bombs.

Throughout the spring of 1943, No.137 Squadron carried on its war on enemy shipping in the Channel. When operating by day it was now usually escorted, sometimes by Spitfires but more often by the Typhoons of the Manston-resident Nos.198 and 609 Squadrons. At night, and by May most of the sorties were at night, single Whirlwinds attacked E-boats, R-boats and minesweepers in the Channel or the adjacent ports, or dropped bombs on marshalling yards or Luftwaffe airfields, notably Poix which received several visits.

The Squadron was now due for re-equipment, and Typhoons were confidently expected; the new CO, Squadron Leader J.B.Wray, arranged for his pilots to get some unofficial Typhoon time with No.609 Squadron - with whom they shared the airfield. However, there was a desperate shortage of Typhoons due to the lack of serviceable Sabre engines and re-equipment with the type was postponed. Apparently No.137 Squadron was due to receive Vultee Vengeance dive-bombers at one stage but this was changed to Hurricane IVs. The Squadron flew to Southend on 12 June 1943 and their Hurricanes began to arrive three days later. Whirlwind operations continued for a short while, the last sorties being flown on the night of 21 June 1943 when Poix was again the target, this time receiving 500-lb bombs, possibly their only operational use on Whirlwinds of the Squadron; the pilots were Squadron Leader J.B.Wray (P7096),

Flight Lieutenant J.M.Bryan (P7047), Flying Officer J.F.Luing (P7046) and Warrant Officer J.H.Ahston (RCAF).

After their withdrawal from No.263 Squadron the RAF could not find any second line use for the remaining Whirlwinds. Their war service with Fighter Command lasted three years during which time the two squadrons carried out just over 5,000 sorties, and achieved a handful of air victories. It was successful against ground targets and small coastal craft but with so few sorties being flown, the monthly average was just 138, its impact on the air war was negligible. Although the type sustained heavy losses in action the Whirlwind did what was asked of it. It could not have been successful in fighter verses fighter combat because it was twin-engined and had been developed to destroy large bomber raids which had ceased by the time it became operational. But could it be so efficient against bombers when it appears that the Whirlwind was vulnerable to bombers' return fire? As a fighter-bomber it obtained more significant results, however it was too late as it was already being overshadowed by the versatile Mosquito. Nevertheless, the Whirlwind sustained exceptional heavy losses. No less than 75% of the Whirlwinds were either lost in action either in accident with the two front-line squadrons, forty-six pilots losing their life. Despite its minimal impact on the war it had an impressive appearance and looks good even now.

A few pilots of No.263 Squadron in Spring 1943. From left to right : Sergeant James I.Simpson, Flight Sergeant Kenneth C.Ridley, Sergeant Donald F.J.Tebbitt, Flight Lieutenant Herbert J.Blackshaw (killed a few days later), Flight Lieutenant Joseph W.E.Holmes, recently posted back from No.137 Squadron, the Canadian Pilot Officer James P.Coyne, and the CO, Squadron Leader Geoffrey B.Warnes. (*Chris Goss*)

No.263 Squadron 25 July 1943 at Warmwell.
L-R back: Sgts W.A.Handley and P.F.Cooper.
Next row : Sgts Kelly and Cole (both groundcrew), F/Sgt Hughes, F/L K.J.F.Funnel, P/O R.C.Hunter, F/Sgt G.A.Wood, F/Sgt R.C.Beaumont, F/Sgt I.D.MacD.Dunlop, Sgts Armstrong and Harvey (both groundcrew),
Sgt D.C.Todd, Sgt Rogers (groundcrew).
Sitting: W/O D.F.J.Tebbitt, F/O J.E.Holman, F/L D.G.Ross, F/O Green (M.O.), F/Sgt Williams (groundcrew), F/L J.P.Coyne (RCAF), S/L E.R.Baker (Squadron's CO), F/L J.E.McClure (RCAF), F/L Owens (Adj), F/O D.E.G.Mogg, F/OAsh (E.O.),
F/O Wordsworth (I.O.).
Sitting front: Sgts G.Williams and W.E.Watkins, F/Sgt J.I.Simpson, Sgt H.M.Proctor. (*Chris Goss*)

Three stalwarts of No.263 Squadron. Left to right, Flying Officer D.A.C. Crooks, Squadron Leader J.G. Munro and Flight Lieutenant T.B.P. Pugh. On 01.04.41 Flying Officer Crooks failed to return from an interception. It was thought he was shot down by the rear gunners onboard a Do.215.
(*D.G. munro via Alex Crawford*)

Some No.263 Squadron pilots pose next to a Whirlwind at Warmwell in the Spring of 1943. Left to right Ken Ridley, Joe Holmes, James 'Sammy' Simpson, Herbert 'Blackie' Blackshaw, Squadron leader Jeff Warnes, James Coyne (RCAF), Donald Tebbit.
(*Westland Helicopter Archives via Fred Ballam*)

The Whirlwind seems not to have been a good candidate for special markings. Expect the airplanes which participated to Operation 'Starkey' in 1943 (left), there is nothing to notice but this unidentified Whirlwind with this shark mouth. Nothing is known about its serial nor its pilot and unit.
(*Westland Helicopter Archives via Fred Ballam - left - and via Chris Thomas - right*)

THE OPERATIONAL RECORD

A rare colour photo of a No.263 Squadron Whirlwind, P7002. The colour scheme and markings give the photo a time span between August 1941 and May 1942. (*Westland Helicopter Archives via Fred Ballam*)

OPERATIONAL DIARY - NUMBER OF SORTIES

Date	137 Sqn	263 Sqn	Tot.
Dec-40	-	30	30
Jan-41	-	63	63
Feb-41	-	72	72
Mar-41	-	182	182
Avr-41	-	179	179
May-41	-	212	212
Jun-41	-	156	156
Jul-41	-	106	106
Aug-41	-	102	102
Sep-41	-	63	63
Oct-41	6	16	22
Nov-41	75	37	112
Dec-41	149	12	161
Jan-42	114	5	119
Feb-42	213	70	283
Mar-42	105	206	311
Avr-42	189	298	487
May-42	255	321	576
Jun-42	195	93	288
Jul-42	245	107	352
Aug-42	110	96	206
Sep-42	22	38	60
Oct-42	52	38	90
Nov-42	54	82	136
Dec-42	72	26	98
Jan-43	75	30	105
Feb-43	47	39	86
Mar-43	52	74	126
Avr-43	87	121	208
May-43	66	92	158
Jun-43	55	10	65
Jul-43	-	16	16
Aug-43	-	104	104
Sep-43	-	80	80
Oct-43	-	84	84
Nov-43	-	94	94
Grand Total	**2,238**	**3,343**	**5,581**

FIRST WHIRLWIND MK.I SORTIES

7 DECEMBER 40
PATROL IN VICINITY OF PLYMOUTH

Serial	Pilot	Up	Down
P6974/Z	S/L H.Eeles	11.55	12.55
P6975/L	F/L W.O.L.Smith	11.55	12.55
P6976/X	F/O J.G.Hugues	11.55	12.55

Claim List of Whirlwind Mk.I Units

Date	Unit	Pilot	SN	Origin	Type	Serial	Conf.	Prob.	Dam.
12.01.41	No.263 Sqn	P/O David Stein	RAF No.84299	RAF	Ju88	P6972	-	-	1
08.02.41	No.263 Sqn	P/O Kenneth A.G. Graham	RAF No.78737	RAF	Ar196	P6969/HE-V	1	-	1
01.03.41	No.263 Sqn	P/O Patrick G. Thornton-Brown	RAF No.81639	RAF	Ju88	P6989	-	-	1
05.03.41	No.263 Sqn	P/O Herbert H. Kitchener	RAF No.87029	RAF	Ju88	P6989	-	-	1
11.03.41	No.263 Sqn	P/O Herbert H. Kitchener	RAF No.87029	RAF	Ju88	P6985/HE-J	-	-	1
01.04.41	No.263 Sqn	S/L Arthur H. Donaldson	RAF No.34150	RAF	Do215	P6998	-	-	1
06.04.41	No.263 Sqn	F/O Bernard Howe	RAF No.33427	RAF	He111	P7002	-	-	0.5
06.04.41	No.263 Sqn	P/O Albert Tooth	RAF No.88469	RAF	He111	P7004	-	-	0.5
06.08.41	No.263 Sqn	P/O Clifford P. Rudland [1]	RAF No.65998	RAF	Bf109	P7002/HE-L	2	-	-
	No.263 Sqn	F/Sgt Robert A. Brackley	RAF No.518164	RAF	Bf109	P6983	-	-	1
	No.263 Sqn	S/L Arthur H. Donaldson	RAF No.34150	RAF	Bf109	P7001	-	1	-
04.09.41	No.263 Sqn	F/O David Stein	RAF No.84299	RAF	Bf109	P6990	1	-	-
07.11.41	No.263 Sqn	Sgt Cecil P. King*	RAF No.958932	RCAF	Bf109	P7112	1	-	-
15.05.42	No.137 Sqn	F/Sgt John R. Brennan	Can./R.72637	RCAF	Ju88	P7111/SF-E	-	-	1
20.06.42	No.137 Sqn	Sgt Joel H. Ashton	Can./R.80070	RCAF	Do217	P7012/SF-V	-	-	0.5
	No.137 Sqn	P/O Charles E. Mercer	Can./J.15738	RCAF	Ju88	P6972	-	-	0.5
06.07.42	No.137 Sqn	F/L Leonard H. Bartlett	RAF No.102959	RAF	Ju88	P7111/SF-E	-	-	0.5
	No.137 Sqn	Sgt Desmond A. Roberts	NZ411994	RNZAF	Ju88	P7037/SF-J	-	-	0.5
25.07.42	No.137 Sqn	P/O John E. McClure	Can./J.15505	RCAF	Ju88	P7104	0.5	-	-
	No.137 Sqn	W/O Robert L. Smith	RAF No.742902	RAF	Ju88	P7102/SF-V	0.5	-	-
29.07.42	No.137 Sqn	F/Sgt James R. Rebbetoy	Can./R.75651	RCAF	Ju88	P7058/SF-G	0.5	-	-
	No.137 Sqn	Sgt Leo O'Neill	RAF No.530323	RAF	Ju88	P7005/SF-H	0.5	-	-
18.08.42	No.137 Sqn	P/O John F. Luing	RAF No.121527	RAF	Ju88	P7055	-	-	0.5
	No.137 Sqn	Sgt Leo O'Neill	RAF No.530323	RAF	Ju88	P7037/SF-J	-	-	0.5
19.08.42	No.137 Sqn	Sgt Alfred E. Brown	RAF No.656417	RAF	Ju88	P6976	1	-	-
	No.137 Sqn	F/O John M. Bryan	RAF No.102570	RAF	Do217	P7121/SF-C	0.5	-	-
	No.137 Sqn	Sgt Desmond A. Roberts	NZ411994	RNZAF	Do217	P7046	0.5	-	-
20.08.42	No.137 Sqn	Sgt John McG. Barclay	RAF No.655794	RAF	Ju88	P6982/SF-S	-	-	1
14.12.42	No.263 Sqn	P/O James P. Coyne	Can./J.15233	RCAF	Fw190	P7057	-	-	1
15.12.42	No.137 Sqn	P/O Robert L. Smith	RAF No.129958	RAF	Fw190	P6976	-	-	1
19.12.42	No.137 Sqn	F/O John M. Bryan	RAF No.102570	RAF	Fw190	P7114	-	0.5	-
	No.137 Sqn	P/O James R. Rebbetoy	Can./J.15741	RCAF	Fw190	P7005/SF-H	-	0.5	-
16.05.43	No.263 Sqn	F/O James P. Coyne	Can./J.15233	RCAF	Fw190	P6974	1	-	-
	No.263 Sqn	P/O Arthur Lee-White**	RAF No.121791	RAF	Fw190	P7059	-	-	1
16.06.43	No.137 Sqn	S/L John B. Wray	RAF No.37874	RAF	Fw190	P7111/SF-E	-	-	1
13.08.43	No.263 Sqn	F/L Ernest R. Baker	RAF No.40660	RAF	Ju88	P7113	1	-	-

Total : 9 aircraft destroyed, 2 probably destroyed, 18 damaged.

* From West Indies.

**From Peru - British parentage.

[1] In two different sorties.

Date	Unit	Pilot	SN	Origin	Serial	Fate
29.12.40	No.263 Sqn	F/L Wynford O.L. SMITH	RAF No.37366	RAF	P6978	†
	No.263 Sqn	P/O Donald M. VINE	RAF No.83718	RAF	P6975/HE-L	†
08.02.41	No.263 Sqn	P/O Kenneth A.G. GRAHAM	RAF No.78737	RAF	P6969/HE-V	†
11.03.41	No.263 Sqn	P/O Herbert H. KITCHENER	RAF No.87029	RAF	P6985/HE-J	-
14.03.41	No.263 Sqn	P/O Patrick G. THORNTON-BROWN	RAF No.81639	RAF	P6988	-
01.04.41	No.263 Sqn	F/L David A.C. CROOKS	RAF No.40678	(CAN)/RAF	P6989	†
04.09.41	No.263 Sqn	Sgt Geoffrey L. BUCKWELL	RAF No.1254477	RAF	P7042	PoW
10.09.41	No.263 Sqn	P/O Denis W. MASON	RAF No.45726	RAF	P7001	†
29.09.41	No.263 Sqn	Sgt Thomas HUNTER	RAF No.1001262	RAF	P7009	†
30.10.41	No.137 Sqn	F/O Colin A.G. CLARK	RAF No.42192	(SA)/RAF	P7091	†
	No.263 Sqn	F/O David STEIN	RAF No.84299	RAF	P7015	PoW
06.11.41	No.263 Sqn	Sgt John J. ROBINSON	RAF No.1057469	RAF	P6970	†
10.11.41	No.137 Sqn	F/Sgt Basil L. ROBERTSON	RAF No.748333	RAF	P6977	-
12.02.42	No.137 Sqn	P/O George W. MARTIN	RAF No.102619	RAF	P7106/SF-D	†
	No.137 Sqn	Sgt John A.W. SANDY	RAF No.1051978	RAF	P7050	†
	No.137 Sqn	W/O Basil L. ROBERTSON	RAF No.748333	RAF	P7107	†
	No.137 Sqn	P/O Ralph O.G. HÄGGBERG	RAF No.120677	(SWE)/RAF	P7093	†
27.05.42	No.137 Sqn	F/Sgt John R. BRENNAN	CAN./R.72637	RCAF	P7122	†
29.05.42	No.137 Sqn	P/O Douglas St.J. JOWITT	RAF No.114169	RAF	P7118	-
27.06.42	No.137 Sqn	P/O Frederick M. FURBER	RAF No.80203	(RHO)/RAF	P7049	-
23.07.42	No.263 Sqn	P/O John J. WALKER	RAF No.119013	RAF	P7060	†
	No.263 Sqn	P/O Vivian L. CURRIE	RAF No.106035	RAF	P7035	†
28.10.42	No.263 Sqn	F/L Arthur N.W. JOHNSTONE	RAF No.42313	RAF	P7014/HE-T	
31.10.42	No.137 Sqn	Sgt F.G. WALDRON	RAF No.1287168	RAF	P7109	PoW
	No.137 Sqn	P/O Douglas St.J.JOWITT	RAF No.114169	RAF	P7115	†
	No.137 Sqn	F/L John E. van SHAICK	RAF No.114086	RAF	P7064	-
07.11.42	No.263 Sqn	P/O Donald R. GILL	CAN./J.15111	RCAF	P7043/HE-A	†
07.12.42	No.263 Sqn	S/L Robert S. WOODWARD	RAF No.74698	RAF	P7105/HE-N	†
	No.263 Sqn	W/O Donald B. McPHAIL	CAN./R.67887	RCAF	P6987	†
22.12.42	No.137 Sqn	Sgt Thomas A. SUTHERLAND	RAF No.655932	RAF	P6998	-
17.01.43	No.137 Sqn	P/O John F. LUING	RAF No.121527	RAF	P7051	-
23.01.43	No.137 Sqn	W/O Alec I. DOIG	RAF No.565057	RAF	P7054	PoW
	No.137 Sqn	Sgt Alfred E. BROWN	RAF No.656417	RAF	P7095/SF-H	†
12.02.43	No.263 Sqn	Sgt David J. WILLIAMS	RAF No.1314587	RAF	P7052	†
18.02.43	No.137 Sqn	Lt Neville A. FREEMAN	SAAF No.19962	SAAF	P7119	†
	No.137 Sqn	P/O Charles E. MERCER	CAN./J.15738	RCAF	P7114	†
02.03.43	No.137 Sqn	Sgt George O.H. WALKER	RAF No.1382117	RAF	P7005/SF-H	PoW
04.04.43	No.137 Sqn	P/O Norbury DUGDALE	RAF No.131147	RAF	P7002/SF-W	-
14.04.43	No.263 Sqn	Sgt John MACAULAY	RAF No.1113286	RAF	P7010	†
16.04.43	No.263 Sqn	F/O Edgar BREARLEY	CAN./J.15157	RCAF	P6995	†
17.04.43	No.263 Sqn	F/O Philip HARVEY	RAF No.102571	(IRE)/RAF	P7090	†
	No.263 Sqn	F/O Cecil P. KING	RAF No.128999	(W.I.)/RAF	P7117/HE-A	†
	No.263 Sqn	F/O Basil C. ABRAMS	RAF No.133547	(SA)/RAF	P7099	†
25.04.43	No.137 Sqn	F/O James R. REBBETOY	CAN./J.15741	RCAF	P7058/SF-G	†
15.05.43	No.263 Sqn	F/L Herbert J. BLACKSHAW	RAF No.111980	RAF	P7094/HE-T	†
18.05.43	No.137 Sqn	F/O Edward L. MUSGRAVE	Aus.403528	RAAF	P7063	†
22.05.43	No.263 Sqn	F/O Arthur LEE-WHITE	RAF No.121791	RAF (1)	P7059	-
23.05.43	No.263 Sqn	P/O Maxwell T. COTTON	Aus.408204	RAAF	P7089	-
15.06.43	No.263 Sqn	P/O Maxwell T. COTTON	Aus.408204	RAAF	P7000	†
22.06.43	No.137 Sqn	Sgt John McG. BARCLAY	RAF No.655794	RAF	P6993	-
23.09.43	No.263 Sqn	F/Sgt George A. WOOD	RAF No.1334647	RAF	P7113	Eva.
08.10.43	No.263 Sqn	F/Sgt James I. SIMPSON	RAF No.656621	RAF	P7047	†
24.10.43	No.263 Sqn	F/O Paul T.R. MERCER	RAF No.127883	RAF	P6979	†
	No.263 Sqn	F/Sgt John GRAY	RAF No.1777605	RAF	P6986	PoW
	No.263 Sqn	F/L David G. ROSS	RAF No.84001	RAF	P6974	-

Total: 55

(1) From Peru, British parentage.

AIRCRAFT LOST BY ACCIDENT

Date	Unit	Pilot	SN	Origin	Serial	Fate
07.08.40	No.263 Sqn	P/O Irving F. McDermott	RAF No.41719	(CAN)/RAF	P6966	-
12.12.40	No.263 Sqn	F/O Alan W.N. Britton	RAF No.72033	RAF	P6980	†
19.01.41	No.263 Sqn	F/L Thomas P. Pugh	RAF No.40137	RAF	P6984/HE-H	-
20.04.41	No.263 Sqn	F/O Bernard Howe	RAF No.33427	RAF	P6992/HE-C	†
30.04.41	No.263 Sqn	P/O George S. Milligan	RAF No.87030	RAF	P7008	†
29.05.41	No.263 Sqn	Sgt Donald F.J. Tebbit	RAF No.951767	RAF	P7006	-
11.06.41	No.263 Sqn	Sgt Reginald G. Pascoe	RAF No.927360	RAF	L6845	†
12.06.41	No.263 Sqn	P/O Roy F. Ferdinand	RAF No.80817	RAF	P7045	†
05.09.41	R-R	*No details available*			P6996	?
09.10.41	No.263 Sqn	F/L Humphrey St-J. Coghlan	AAF No.90117	RAF	P6999	-
	No.263 Sqn	P/O Ormonde J.H. Hoskins	RAF No.69485	RAF	P6968	†
28.10.41	No.137 Sqn	S/L John Sample	AAF No.90278	RAF	P7053	†
14.12.41	No.263 Sqn	Sgt Derrick E. Prior	RAF No.1166018	RAF	P7044	†
03.01.42	No.263 Sqn	-	-	-	P7038	-
07.03.42	No.263 Sqn	Sgt Peter A. Jardine	RAF No.711019	(SA)/RAF	P7039	-
09.03.42	No.137 Sqn	P/O Charles W. De-Shane	Can./J.15148	RCAF	P7036/SF-X	†
19.03.42	No.263 Sqn	P/O Vivian L. Currie	RAF No.106158	RAF	P7004	-
01.04.42	No.263 Sqn	P/O Philip Harvey	RAF No.102571	(IRE)/RAF	P7112	-
02.04.42	No.263 Sqn	-	-	-	P7041	-
04.05.42	No.137 Sqn	P/O Robert E.D. Wright	Can./J.15147	RCAF	P7103	†
30.06.42	No.137 Sqn	-	-	-	P7101/SF-A	-
21.09.42	No.263 Sqn	Sgt Peter A. Jardine	RAF No.711019	(SA)/RAF	P7003	†
28.10.42	No.263 Sqn	F/L James R. Cooksey	RAF No.44263	RAF	P7120	-
13.01.43	No.137 Sqn	Sgt Edmund A. Bolster	RAF No.1090706	RAF	P7061	-
09.02.43	No.263 Sqn	Sgt John Macauley	RAF No.1113286	RAF	P6991	-
19.02.43	No.263 Sqn	F/Sgt Francis L. Hicks	Aus.408207	RAAF	P7062/HE-L	†
30.03.43	No.137 Sqn	P/O John T. Davidson	RAF No.114577	RAF	P7104	-
15.04.43	No.137 Sqn	P/O John M. Hadow	RAF No.122121	RAF	P7121/SF-C	-
01.05.43	No.137 Sqn	Sgt Aubrey C. Smith	RAF No.1340628	RAF	P6976	-
07.05.43	No.263 Sqn	Sgt John Thould	RAF No.1246400	RAF	P7057	-
13.07.43	No.263 Sqn	Sgt Leonard J. Knott	RAF No.1386897	RAF	P7110	-
01.08.43	No.263 Sqn	Sgt Peter F. Cooper	RAF No.1477083	RAF	P6981	-
10.09.43	No.263 Sqn	S/L Ernest R. Baker	RAF No.40660	RAF	P7096	-
08.01.44	No.3 FP	F/O Douglas J. Cooper		RAF	P7097	-

Total: 34

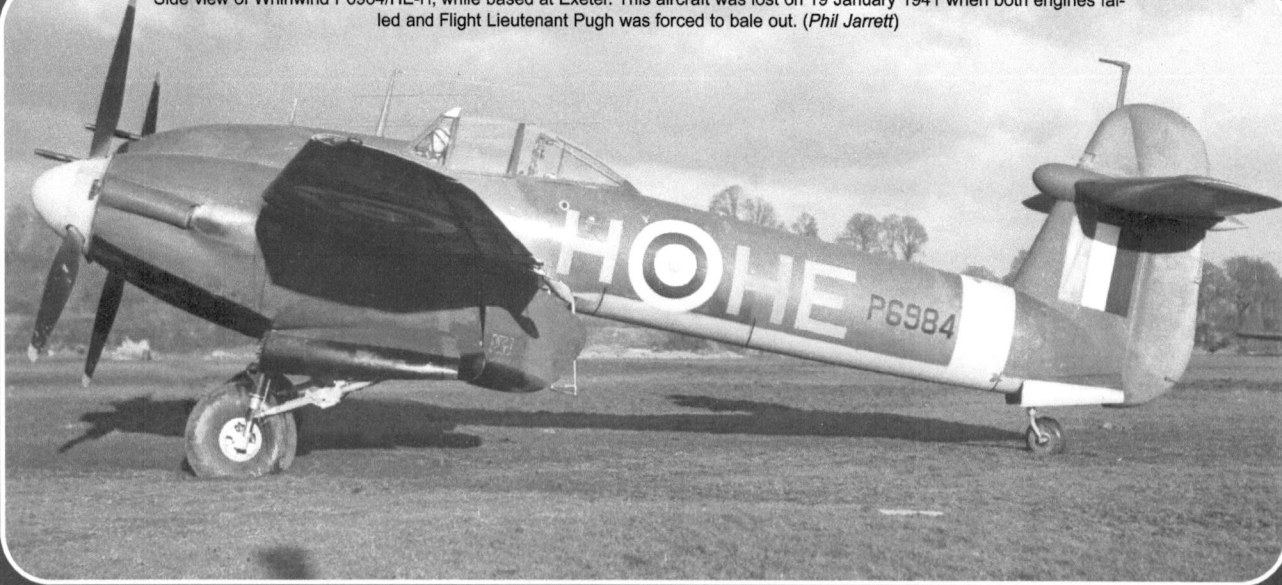

Side view of Whirlwind P6984/HE-H, while based at Exeter. This aircraft was lost on 19 January 1941 when both engines failed and Flight Lieutenant Pugh was forced to bale out. (*Phil Jarrett*)

SERIALS		DATE ON SQN	DATE OFF SQN
L6845 :	25 Sqn	30.05.40	07.07.40
	263 Sqn	07.07.40	16.10.40
	263 Sqn	30.03.41	07.04.41
	263 Sqn	03.06.41	11.06.41
P6966 :	263 Sqn	05.07.40	07.08.40
P6967 :	25 Sqn	17.06.40	07.07.40
	263 Sqn	07.07.40	23.09.40
	137 Sqn	31.12.42	09.04.43
P6968 :	263 Sqn	18.07.40	09.10.41
P6969 :	263 Sqn [HE-V]	18.07.40	08.02.41
P6970 :	263 Sqn	26.07.40	06.11.41
P6971 :	263 Sqn	31.08.40	25.10.41
	137 Sqn	04.09.42	27.12.42
	263 Sqn	27.12.42	19.10.43
P6972 :	263 Sqn	01.09.40	30.03.41
	137 Sqn	06.11.41	08.07.42
P6973 :	263 Sqn	17.09.40	05.07.41
P6974 :	263 Sqn [HE-Z in 1940 and HE-X later]	07.09.40	01.09.43
P6975 :	263 Sqn [HE-L]	21.10.40	29.12.40
P6976 :	263 Sqn [HE-X]	07.11.40	15.02.41
	137 Sqn	20.02.42	01.05.43
P6977 :	263 Sqn	07.11.40	01.11.41
	137 Sqn	01.11.41	11.11.41
P6978 :	263 Sqn	12.11.40	29.12.40
P6979 :	263 Sqn [HE-G]	07.11.40	11.11.41
	263 Sqn	29.06.42	24.10.43
P6980 :	263 Sqn	07.12.40	12.12.40
P6981 :	263 Sqn [HE-B]	07.12.40	16.02.42
	137 Sqn	16.02.42	04.05.42
	263 Sqn	08.04.43	01.08.43
P6982 :	263 Sqn	26.11.40	01.09.41
	137 Sqn [SF-P]	07.02.42	26.05.42
P6983 :	263 Sqn	07.12.40	03.01.42
	137 Sqn	16.02.42	22.06.42
	263 Sqn	18.08.43	11.01.44
P6984 :	263 Sqn [HE-H]	22.12.40	29.01.41
P6985 :	263 Sqn [HE-J]	03.01.41	24.03.41
P6986 :	263 Sqn	04.01.41	24.11.41
	137 Sqn	13.09.42	18.10.42
	263 Sqn [HE-G]*	21.10.42	16.02.43
	137 Sqn	16.02.43	24.06.43
	263 Sqn	24.06.43	24.10.43
P6987 :	263 Sqn [HE-L until March 41]	04.01.41	19.11.41
	263 Sqn [HE-I]	05.06.42	07.12.42
P6988 :	263 Sqn	04.01.41	14.03.41
P6989 :	263 Sqn [HE-C]*	19.01.41	01.04.41
P6990 :	263 Sqn	09.01.41	18.12.42
	263 Sqn	28.05.43	19.11.43
P6991 :	263 Sqn [HE-R until March 42]	06.02.41	09.02.43
P6992 :	263 Sqn [HE-C]	13.02.41	21.04.41
P6993 :	263 Sqn [HE-S]	13.02.41	29.05.41
	137 Sqn [SF-A]	23.07.42	22.06.43
P6994§ :	263 Sqn	13.02.41	01.11.41
P6995 :	263 Sqn	18.03.41	09.05.41
	263 Sqn	06.07.42	17.04.43
P6996 :	263 Sqn	13.02.41	28.08.41
P6997 :	137 Sqn	26.01.43	24.06.43

Sergeant George Walker was posted missing after an abortive mission due to bad weather on 02.03.43. Walker enventually made a force-landing to becaome a PoW. His aircraft is seen here being inspected by German officers. (*ww2images*)

Below:
James Patrick Coyne (RCAF) is posing in P7094/HE-T, probably in May 1943. It was Flight Lieutenant H.J. Blackshaw's regular mount, and both were lost a few days later. (*Phil Jarrett*)

Above:
Two views of P6976/HE-X after its accident in February 1941. The Whirlwind was repaired and stored at No.18 MU in August 1941 and eventually was alloted to No.137 Squadron in February 1942. (*Chris Goss*).

Upper right:
P7011/SF-U at Manston in 1943.
(via Chris Thomas)

Below right:
P7043/HE-A in Autumn 1942. This Whirlwind was one of the first Whirlwinds to become a "Whirlibombers". Being the mount of Flight Lieutenant G.B.Warnes, it was eventually lost with his pilot, Pilot Officer D.R.Gill (RCAF) a few weeks later. *(Jerry Brewer)*

	263 Sqn	24.06.43	11.01.44
P6998 :	263 Sqn	25.02.41	16.10.41
	137 Sqn	13.09.42	22.12.42
P6999 :	263 Sqn	27.03.41	09.10.41
P7000 :	263 Sqn	01.03.41	15.06.41
	263 Sqn	18.03.42	15.06.43
P7001 :	263 Sqn	13.04.41	10.09.41
P7002 :	263 Sqn [HE-L]	13.03.41	21.12.41
	137 Sqn [SF-W]	02.02.43	04.04.43
P7003 :	263 Sqn	01.05.41	21.09.42
P7004 :	263 Sqn	13.03.41	19.03.42
P7005 :	263 Sqn [HE-A]	05.04.41	07.05.41
	137 Sqn [SF-H]	08.03.42	02.03.43
P7006 :	263 Sqn	16.04.41	29.05.41
P7007 :	263 Sqn	29.03.41	13.08.43
P7008 :	263 Sqn	15.04.41	30.04.41
P7009 :	263 Sqn	22.04.41	29.09.41
P7010 :	263 Sqn	25.01.43	14.04.43
P7011 :	263 Sqn [HE-H at a time]	13.05.41	06.06.42
	137 Sqn [SF-U]	07.11.42	24.06.43
	263 Sqn	24.11.43	08.02.44
P7012 :	137 Sqn [SF-V]	15.11.41	24.06.43
	263 Sqn	24.06.43	11.01.44
P7013 :	263 Sqn	04.05.41	16.10.41
	263 Sqn	18.04.42	04.11.43
P7014 :	263 Sqn [HE-T]	15.05.42	28.10.42
P7015 :	263 Sqn	15.10.41	30.10.41
P7035 :	137 Sqn	26.09.41	05.04.42
	263 Sqn	05.04.42	23.07.42
P7036 :	137 Sqn [SF-X]	28.09.41	09.03.42
P7037 :	137 Sqn [SF-J]	20.09.41	15.10.42
	263 Sqn	10.10.43	08.02.44
P7038 :	137 Sqn	26.09.41	01.12.41
	263 Sqn	01.12.41	03.01.42
P7039 :	263 Sqn	11.06.41	07.03.43
P7040 :	263 Sqn	08.03.43	10.02.44
P7041 :	263 Sqn	27.05.41	02.04.42
P7042 :	263 Sqn	20.06.41	04.09.41
P7043 :	263 Sqn [HE-A]	21.05.42	07.11.42
P7044 :	263 Sqn	15.06.41	15.12.41
P7045 :	263 Sqn	08.06.41	12.06.41
P7046 :	263 Sqn	15.06.41	29.08.41
	137 Sqn	16.02.42	24.06.43
	263 Sqn	24.06.43	08.02.44
P7047 :	137 Sqn	11.04.43	13.07.43
	263 Sqn	13.07.43	08.10.43
P7048 :	137 Sqn	27.11.41	31.05.43
P7049 :	137 Sqn	22.09.41	11.07.42
P7050 :	137 Sqn	28.09.41	12.02.42
P7051 :	263 Sqn	16.06.41	22.05.42
	137 Sqn	04.09.42	18.01.43
P7052 :	263 Sqn	05.11.41	12.02.43
P7053 :	137 Sqn	28.09.41	28.10.41
P7054 :	137 Sqn	11.02.42	15.06.42
	263 Sqn	30.05.42	03.06.42
	137 Sqn	03.06.42	23.01.43
P7055 :	"BELLOWS ARGENTINA No.1". 137 Sqn	01.11.41	03.09.42
	137 Sqn [SF-S]	18.02.43	24.06.43
	263 Sqn	24.06.43	18.01.44
P7056 :	"THE PRIDE OF YEOVIL". 263 Sqn	06.10.41	18.12.42
	137 Sqn	14.04.43	27.06.43

	263 Sqn	27.06.43	30.08.43
P7057 :	137 Sqn	28.09.41	11.01.42
	263 Sqn	14.07.42	08.05.43
P7058 :	137 Sqn [SF-G at a time]	28.09.41	25.04.43
P7059 :	263 Sqn	01.08.42	22.05.43
P7060 :	263 Sqn	30.12.41	23.07.42
P7061 :	263 Sqn [HE-A]	19.09.41	22.05.42
	137 Sqn	07.11.42	14.01.43
P7062 :	137 Sqn	20.09.41	21.01.42
	263 Sqn [HE-L]	18.07.42	19.02.43
P7063 :	263 Sqn	20.09.41	16.03.42
	137 Sqn	16.03.42	18.05.43
P7064 :	137 Sqn [SF-G at a time]	18.11.41	31.10.42
P7089 :	263 Sqn	10.10.41	23.05.43
P7090 :	137 Sqn	22.09.41	05.04.42
	263 Sqn	05.04.42	18.11.42
	263 Sqn	26.03.43	18.04.43
P7091 :	137 Sqn	22.09.41	30.10.41
P7092 :	137 Sqn [SF-Q at a time]	17.10.41	31.01.42
	137 Sqn [SF-U]	04.09.42	27.06.43
	263 Sqn [HE-D]	27.06.43	22.01.44
P7093 :	137 Sqn [SF-A]	07.01.42	12.02.42
P7094 :	"BELLOWS". 137 Sqn	20.09.41	31.12.41
	137 Sqn	22.09.42	08.10.42
	263 Sqn [HE-S then HE-T in May 43]	08.10.42	16.05.43
P7095 :	137 Sqn [SF-H]	22.06.42	23.01.43
P7096 :	137 Sqn	30.09.41	27.02.42
	137 Sqn	03.01.43	27.06.43
	263 Sqn	27.06.43	14.08.43
P7097 :	137 Sqn	06.11.41	20.02.42
	263 Sqn	30.05.43	11.01.44
P7098 :	137 Sqn [SF-P for a short time]	17.04.42	27.06.43
	263 Sqn	27.06.43	10.01.44
P7099 :	263 Sqn	30.07.41	17.04.43
P7100 :	263 Sqn	05.12.41	17.04.42
	263 Sqn	04.11.43	29.01.44
P7101 :	137 Sqn [SF-A]	18.04.42	04.07.42
P7102 :	"COMRADES IN ARMS". 137 Sqn [SF-P]	22.06.42	25.01.43
	263 Sqn [HE-N]	14.09.43	29.01.44
P7103 :	137 Sqn	27.11.41	04.05.42
P7104 :	137 Sqn	14.04.42	30.03.43
P7105 :	137 Sqn	23.09.41	21.01.42
	263 Sqn [HE-N]	12.08.42	07.12.42
P7106 :	137 Sqn [SF-D]	20.09.41	12.02.42
P7107 :	137 Sqn	20.09.41	12.02.42
P7108 :	263 Sqn	15.12.41	20.02.42
	263 Sqn	27.02.43	08.02.44
P7109 :	137 Sqn	15.11.41	31.10.42
P7110 :	263 Sqn [HE-E, HE-G & HE-H at a time]	15.10.41	13.07.43
P7111 :	"BELLOWS URUGUAY No.2". 137 Sqn [SF-E]	13.03.42	04.07.43
	263 Sqn [SF-W]	04.07.43	11.01.44
P7112 :	263 Sqn	15.10.41	01.04.42
P7113 :	263 Sqn	09.11.42	23.09.43
P7114 :	263 Sqn	05.11.41	19.07.42
	263 Sqn	22.09.42	17.11.42
	137 Sqn	17.11.42	19.02.43
P7115 :	137 Sqn	16.09.42	31.10.42
P7116 :	"BELLOWS ARGENTINA No.2"		
	263 Sqn [HE-F], [HE-J in June 42]	03.11.41	18.12.42
P7117 :	"BELLOWS ARGENTINA No.3"		
	263 Sqn [HE-E in Nov-41] [HE-A in April 43]	03.11.41	18.04.43

P7118 :	"BELLOWS ARGENTINA No.4". 137 Sqn	20.02.42	29.05.42
P7119 :	"BELLOWS ARGENTINA No.5". 137 Sqn	08.03.42	19.02.43
P7120 :	"BELLOWS ARGENTINA No.6". 263 Sqn [HE-R in Jul.42]	26.02.42	28.10.42
P7121 :	"BELLOWS ARGENTINA No.7". 137 Sqn [SF-C]	06.02.42	16.04.43
P7122 :	"BELLOWS URUGUAY No.1". 137 Sqn	13.03.42	27.05.42

*Unsure.

Note : Presentation aircraft "Bellows Uruguay III, Condor II and Pride of Yeovil II, III and IV" are not identified, but believed to have been funded.

Left:
A line up of Whirlwinds at Fairlight Common. HE-A was P7061, while HE-X may have been either P6974 or P6976.
(Westland Helicopter Archives via Fred Ballam)

Left:
Although declared 'Category B' after being struck by Lysander N1249 while parked at Matlask on 30 June 1942, Whirlwind SF-A, P7101, was never repaired.
(J.Gates)

Left:
Westland Whirlwind Mk.I P7062, of No.263 Squadron flown by Pilot Officer William A. Lovell, (RCAF), taken during a routine flight in July 1942.
William Lovell was an English-born American who was transferred
to USAAF a few weeks later.
(Phil Jarrett)

ROLL OF HONOUR

WHIRLWIND MK.I

Name	Rank	Age	Origin	Date	Serial
ABRAMS, Basil Courtney	F/O	n/k	(SA)/RAF	18.04.43	P7099
BLACKSHAW, Herbert John	F/L	26	RAF	16.05.43	P7094
BREARLEY, Edgar	F/O	26	RCAF	17.04.43	P6995
BRENNAN, John Robert	F/Sgt	19	RCAF	27.05.42	P7122
BRITTON, Allan Walter Nayler	F/O	23	RAF	12.12.40	P6980
BROWN, Alfred Edward	Sgt	27	RAF	23.01.43	P7095
CLARK, Colin Anthony Gordon	F/O	28	(SA)/RAF	30.10.41	P7091
COTTON, Maxwell Tylney	P/O	22	RAAF	15.06.43	P7000
CROOKS, David Alexander Cummings	F/L	28	(CAN)/RAF	01.04.41	P6989
CURRIE, Vivian Lester	P/O	22	RAF	23.07.42	P7035
DE-SHANE, Charles Wilbert	P/O	20	RCAF	09.03.42	P7036
FERDINAND, Roy Frederick	P/O	21	RAF	12.06.41	P7045
FREEMAN, Neville Austin	Lt	21	SAAF	18.02.43	P7119
GILL, Donald Ross	F/O	27	RCAF	07.11.42	P7043
GRAHAM, Kenneth Alfred George	P/O	20	RAF	08.02.41	P6969
HÄGGBERG, Ralph Otto Gustav	P/O	19	(SWE)/RAF	12.02.42	P7093
HARVEY, Philip	F/O	23	(IRE)/RAF	18.04.43	P7090
HICKS, Francis Leslie	F/Sgt	30	RAAF	19.02.43	P7062
HOSKINS, Ormonde John Horace	P/O	26	RAF	09.10.41	P6968
HOWE, Bernard	F/O	22	RAF	20.04.41	P6992
HUNTER, Thomas	Sgt	21	RAF	20.09.41	P7009
JARDINE, Peter Alastair	Sgt	20	(SA)/RAF	21.09.42	P7003
JOWITT, Douglas St.John	P/O	n/a	RAF	28.10.42	P7115
KING, Cecil Percy	F/O	23	(W.I)/RAF	17.04.43	P7117
MACAULEY, John	Sgt	23	RAF	14.04.43	P7010
MARTIN, George William	P/O	n/k	RAF	12.02.42	P7106
MASON, Dennis William	P/O	23	RAF	10.09.41	P7001
McPHAIL, Donald Burton	W/O	25	RCAF	07.12.42	P6987
MERCER, Charles Eldred	P/O	24	RCAF	18.02.43	P7114
MERCER, Paul Thomas Richard	F/O	n/k	RAF	24.10.43	P6979
MILLIGAN, George Stanley	P/O	22	RAF	30.04.41	P7008
MUSGRAVE, Edward Lancelot	F/O	25	RAAF	18.05.43	P7063
PASCOE, Reginald Gunn	Sgt	20	RAF	11.06.41	L6845
PRIOR, Derrick Ellis	Sgt	21	RAF	14.12.41	P7044
REBBETOY, James Reginald	F/O	26	RCAF	25.04.43	P7058
ROBERTSON, Basil Lionell	W/O	20	RAF	12.02.42	P7107
ROBINSON, John Joseph	Sgt	21	RAF	06.11.41	P6970
SAMPLE, John	S/L	28	RAF	28.10.41	P7053
SANDY, John Anthony William	Sgt	n/a	RAF	12.02.42	P7050
SIMPSON, James Ian	P/O	24	RAF	08.10.43	P7047
SMITH, Wynford Ormonde Leoni	F/Sgt	25	RAF	29.12.40	P6978
VINE, Donald Martin	P/O	23	RAF	29.12.40	P6975
WALKER, John James	P/O	22	RAF	23.07.42	P7060
WILLIAMS, David John	Sgt	20	RAF	12.02.43	P7052
WOODWARD, Robert Sinckler	S/L	23	RAF	07.12.42	P7105
WRIGHT, Robert Elmer Douglas	P/O	26	RCAF	04.05.42	P7103

Total: 46

n/k : not known

Armourers re-arming the four 20mm cannons with the drum magazines with below the camera gun. (*Phil Jarrett*)

Westland Whirlwind Mk.I P6969, No.263 Squadron, Exeter, United Kingdom, Summer 1940.
Fourth production Whirlwind, P6969 was one of the first Whirlwind to be taken of charge by No.263
Sqn in July 1940. It is seen here later in summer that year with the standard camouflage and markings. Note the already faded paints in some parts. This aircraft had eventually a short career as it
was shot down on 08.02.41. Its pilot Kenneth Graham claimed the first Whirlwind victory but was
also shot down and killed by the return fire from the rear gunner. (see photo p.7)

**Westland Whirlwind Mk.I P6987, No.263 Squadron, Exeter, United Kingdom, January-
February 1941.**
P6987 was delivered direct from Westland to 263 Sqn on 04.01.41, with camouflage and markings
in force within Fighter Command at that time introduced at the end of 1940. In November that year
it had a Cat.B accident, was repaired and was sent for storage at No.51.MU on 02.04.42. It was
issued again to the squadron on 05.06.42 and eventually shot down by flak on 07.12.42 off Jersey.
Its pilot, Donald McPhail (RCAF) was killed. (see photo p.6)

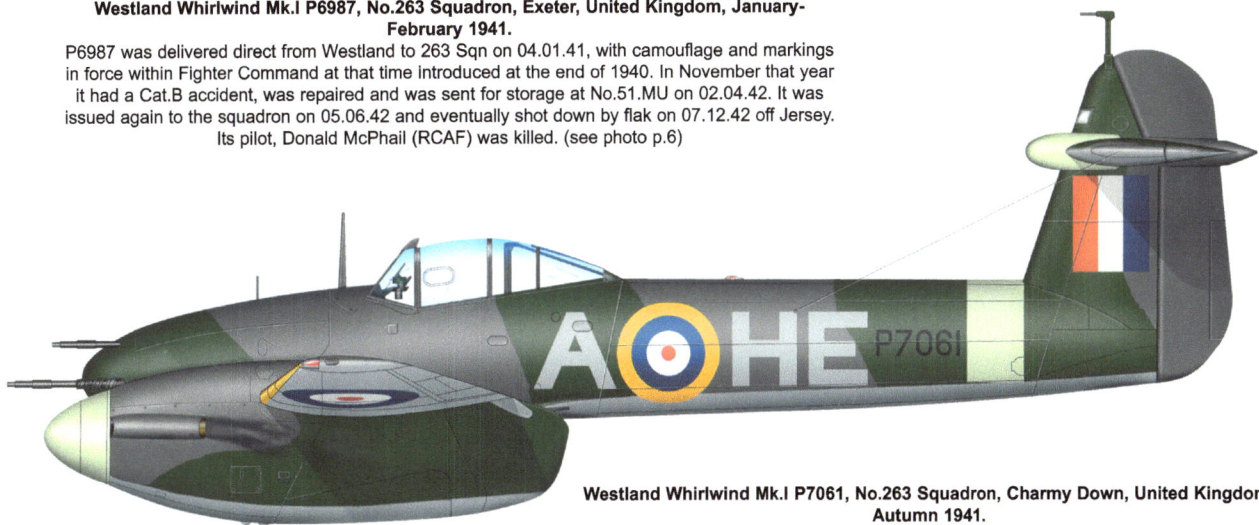

**Westland Whirlwind Mk.I P7061, No.263 Squadron, Charmy Down, United Kingdom,
Autumn 1941.**
P7041 was taken on charge at No.39 MU on 25.05.41 and was issued to No.263 Sqn on
19.09.41 with the new Ocean Grey/Dark Green camouflage. In May 1942 he sent to Westland
for an overhaul and was stored from August 1942. On 07.11.42 it was issued to No.137 Sqn
and served with this unit until suffering a Cat.B accident (Sgt Edmund Bolster) on 13.01.43.
However after investigation, the aircraft was declared Cat.E and SOC. (see photo p.32)

Westland Whirlwind Mk.I P6982, No.137 Squadron, Matlask, February 1942.
P6982 was issued direct from factory to No.263 Sqn on 26.11.40 with which It served until September 1941 when it returned to Westland either for overhaul either for repairs. Subsequently, it was sent to No.51 MU in December 1941 painted with the Day Fighter Scheme. On 07.02.42, it was issued to No.137 Sqn when on 26th May it was damaged in a Cat.B accident. P6982 was repaired and stored at No.18 MU from 07.09.42 onwards and was never issued again to any flying unit being eventually scrapped on 30.09.44. This aircraft was flown by many pilots during its short career with No.137 Sqn, with no less than 15 names associated with this aircraft in 32 sorties.

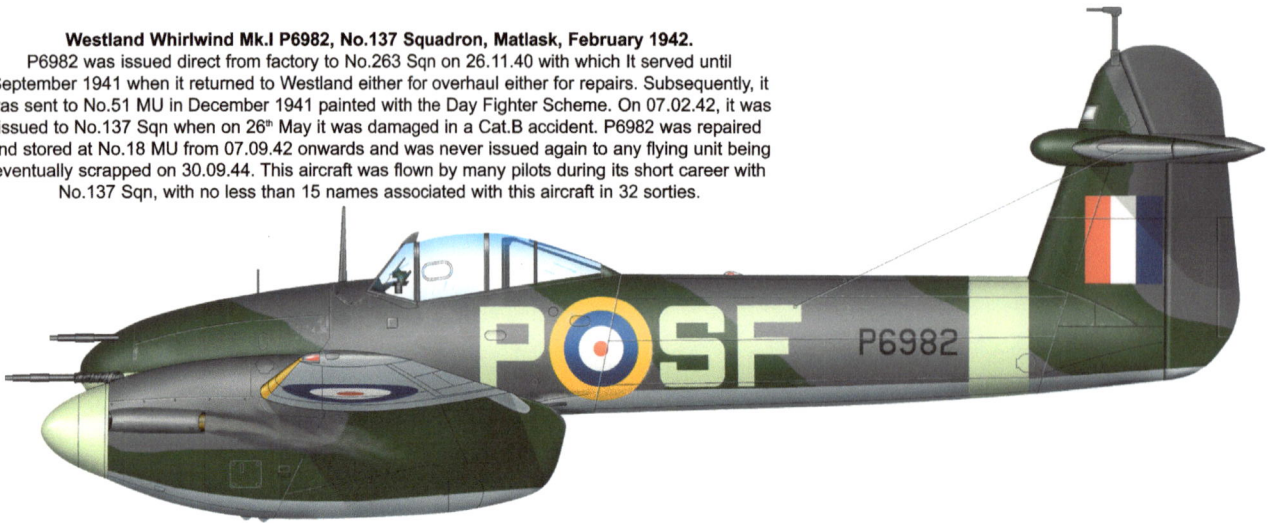

Westland Whirlwind Mk.I P7116, No.263 Squadron, Squadron Leader Thomas P. Pugh, Colerne, United Kingdom, January 1942.
Delivered to No.39 MU on 27.10.41, P7116 was issued to No.263 Sqn on 03.11.41 to become the CO's regular mount. It is painted with the new Day Fighter Scheme. P7116 served during one year with the Squadron until being used by the Station Flight Colerne between December 1942 and March 1943. Following a minor accident P7116 was sent to Westland on 26.03.43 for some repairs which were not carried out, believed due to unexpected corrosion and P7116 was finally SOC on 01.05.43. P7116 was one of the Whirlwinds the most interesting regarding the artworks. (See photo p.10)

Westland Whirlwind Mk.I P7062, No.263 Squadron, Pilot Officer William A.Lovell (RCAF), Angle, United Kingdom, July 1942.
Taken on charge on 28.06.41 at No.39 MU, P7062 was first issued to No.137 Sqn in September 1941 among the first Whirlwinds allotted to this unit. It was damaged in an accident on 07.01.42 and was sent for repairs. It was stored a short time at No.18 MU in July 1942 and was eventually issued to No.263 Sqn on 18th. It was lost on 19.02.43 during Army exercises on the Wroughton-Swindon Road killing its pilot, F/Sgt Francis Hicks (RAAF). William Lovell was an English-born American who was transferred to USAAF a few weeks later and seems to have flown regulary this aircraft.

Westland Whirlwind Mk.I P7043, No.263 Squadron, Flight Lieutenant Geoffrey B. Warnes, Warmwell, United Kingdom, Autumn 1942.
P7043 was taken on charge on 12.05.41 at No.18 MU. Nine days later it was issued to No.263 Sqn and by autumn 1942, P7043 had become more or less the regular mount of Geoffrey Warnes, but it is not sure that the personal artwork was his own one. The aircraft was lost with its pilot of the day (Donald Gill - RCAF) a couple a weeks later on 07.11.42 during a *Rhubarb* operation. P7043 had logged 68.7 hours only. Note the small size of the serial. The colours of the part ahead the stabilizators are believed to be black and yellow. (see photo p.29)

Westland Whirlwind Mk.I P7094 *"Bellows"*, No.263 Squadron, Flight Lieutenant Herbert J. Blackshaw, Warmwell, United Kingdom, May 1943.
Taken on charge by No.51 MU on 17.07.41, P7094 was first issued to No.137 Sqn on 20.09.41. On 23.12.41 it suffered a Cat.B accident and was sent for repairs and sent later at No.18 MU from 07.09.42 before to be issued again to No.137 Sqn two weeks later. It was eventually issued to No.263 Sqn on 08.10.42. Suffering another Cat.B accident in April 1943 it was sent again to Westland for repairs. It returned to No.263 Sqn on 02.05.43 but was lost in operations on the 15th with its pilot, F/L Blackshaw. Point of interest, this aircraft seems to have been camouflaged using three paints, Dark Green, Ocean Grey (or possibly a light mixed grey), and areas of a dark mixed grey. See photo p28. The photo was probably taken when the aircraft was collected at Westlands in early May 1943. P7094 had flown 165.7 hours.

Westland Whirlwind Mk.I P7037, No.137 Squadron, Manston, United Kingdom, October 1942.
P7037 is seen here when it suffered a Cat.AC accident in October 1942 (see photo p.19). Taken on charge on 28.04.41 at No.39 MU it was flying at the squadron since September 1941. Repaired it stayed at Westland for a while before being sent for storage at No.18 MU on 08.09.43. It was issued to No.263 Sqn one month later. In February 1944 he was issued to No.18 MU where it remained before being SOC on 30.09.44.

Westland Whirlwind Mk.I P7092, No.137 Squadron, Manston, United Kingdom, Spring 1943.
P7092 was taken on charge at No.51 MU on 06.07.41. The following month it was issued to No.137 Sqn (17.10.41). It was sent to Westland for repairs after a Cat.B accident in January 1942 and was stored at No.18 MU between July and September 1942 before returning to No.137 Sqn. It is seen here at the end of its career with the squadron as it was issued to No.263 Sqn on 27.06.43 with which it served before being withdrawn from use on 31.12.43. It was SOC soon afterwards on 22.01.44.

Westland Whirlwind Mk.I P7111 "Bellows Uruguay No.2", No.137 Squadron, Matlask, United Kingdom, Summer 1942.
P7111 was taken on charge at No.39 MU on 28.01.42. It was issued to No.137 Sqn on 13.03.42 and served over more a year with this unit before being taken on charge by No.263 Sqn on 04.07.43. By summer 1942, this aircraft was usually flown by Flight Lieutenant Leonard H. Bartlett before he left to become the CO of No.253 Sqn in September. Note that the name 'Bellows Uruguay No.2' seems to have been first painted on a Dark Earth paint and left like this when P7111 was re-painted with Ocean Grey paint.

Westland Whirlwind Mk.I P7111 "Bellows Uruguay No.2", No.263 Squadron, Warmwell, United Kingdom, Summer 1943.
P7111 is seen here, a few months later, whilst serving with No.263 Squadron. The aircraft having been sent a few times for repairs at Westland, P7111 may have received a new paint as only "Bellows" was written in yellow below the cockpit. Note the personal artwork, one of the few notices on a Whirlwind. P7111 served until the squadron converted onto the Typhoon in December and was SOC in January 1944.

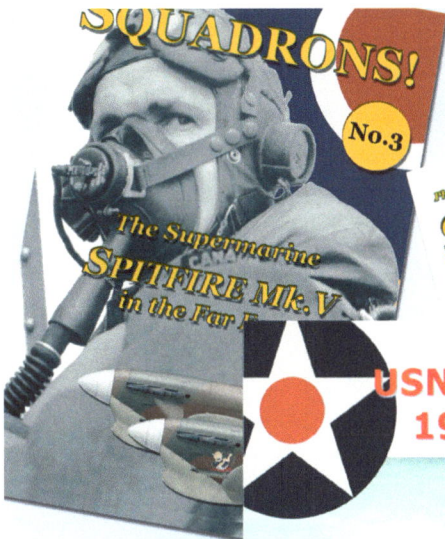

SQUADRONS!

No.3

The Supermarine
SPITFIRE Mk.V
in the Far E

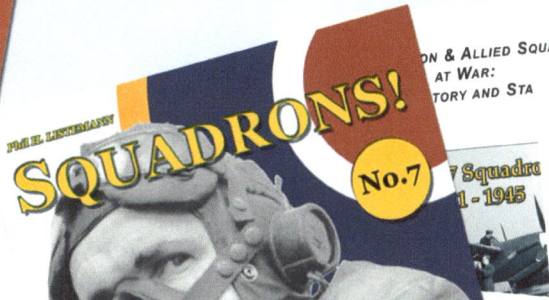

Phil H. LISTEMANN

SQUADRONS!

No.7

The Supermarine
SPITFIRE F.21

RAF, DOMINION & ALLIED SQUADRONS
AT WAR:
HISTORY AND STA

7 Squadro
1 - 1945

RAF, DOMINION & ALLIED SQUADRONS
AT WAR:
Study, History and Statistics

No.309 (Polish) Squadron
1940 - 1947

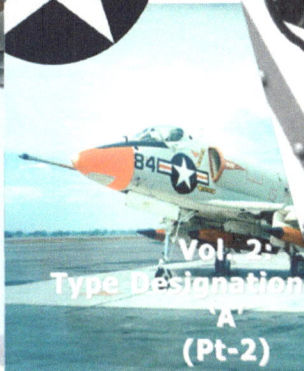

USN
19

Vol. 2:
Type-Designation
'A'
(Pt-2)

Phil H. LISTEMANN

SQUADRONS!

No.2

e Republic
Thunderbolt Mk.I

ZT

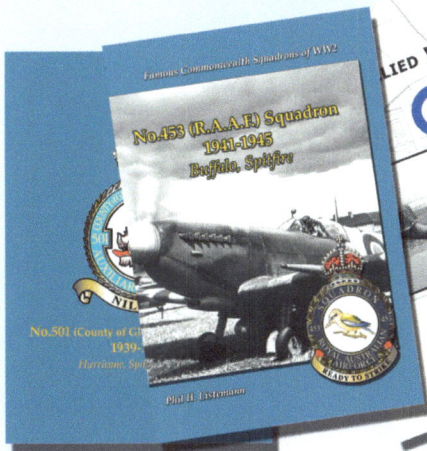

Famous Commonwealth Squadrons of WW2

No.453 (R.A.A.F) Squadron
1941-1945
Buffalo, Spitfire

No.501 (County of Gl
1939-
Hurricane, Sp

Phil H. Listemann

www.RAF-IN-COMBAT.com

- USN Aircraft 1922-1962 -
- Squadrons! -
- RAF, Dominion and Allied squadrons at War -
- Allied Wings -
- Famous squadrons of WW2 -

RAF, DOMINION & ALLIED SQUA
AT WAR:
Study, History and Stati:

LIED WINGS

No.16

Short SINGAPORE III
Phil H. LISTEMANN

No.131 (County of Kent) S
1941-1945

ALLIED WINGS

No.18

The Supermarine SPITFIRE
F.24
Phil H. LISTEMANN

ALLIED WINGS

No.12

The Curtiss SBC in
French service
Phil H. LISTEMANN

www.ingramcontent.com/pod-product-compliance
Lightning Source LLC
LaVergne TN
LVHW072115070426
835510LV00002B/60